Planning the Location of Urban-Suburban Rail Lines: An Application of Cost-Benefit and Optimal Path Analysis

Planning the Location of Urban-Suburban Rail Lines: An Application of Cost-Benefit and Optimal Path Analysis

Glenn D. Westley

Ballinger Publishing Company • Cambridge, Massachusetts
A Subsidiary of J.B. Lippincott Company

International Standard Book Number: 0-88410-668-3

Library of Congress Catalog Card Number: 78-6476

Printed in the United States of America

Library of Congress Cataloging in Publication Data

Westley, Glenn D
  Planning the location of urban-suburban rail lines.

  1. Electric railroads—Location—Cost effectiveness. 2. Street-railroads—Location—Cost effectiveness. 3. Local transit—Mathematical models. I. Title.
HE5361.W47   388.4'2   78-6476
ISBN 0-88410-668-3

Acknowledgments

Many people have given assistance throughout the long period of creating this book. Because of their help, advice, and encouragement these pages are better than what I alone could have produced. Deserving of mention are F. Gerard Adams, W. Bruce Allen, Eileen Argulewicz, Eva Duvdevani, Judith Helzner, Jeanne Holzgrefe, Eleanor Howard, Gerald Jaynes, Eileen Kraus, Stephen Ross, Emery Simon, D. Tomasello, and Michelle White. None are to be held responsible for any errors that may remain.

To Jeannie, who endured without complaint all of those lost weekends

Contents

List of Figures

List of Tables

Planning the Location of Urban-Suburban Rail Lines: An Application of Cost-Benefit and Optimal Path Analysis

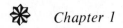

The Optimal Rail Problem

Dynamic systems in economics range at least as far back into history as Adam Smith's model of economic growth, described in rather nonquantitative terms in *The Wealth of Nations*. Dynamics remained submerged, however, throughout the next century—in which the arguments of Ricardo, Mill, Walras, Edgeworth, and others took center stage. Marx was the stellar exception to this hundred years of statics, but even Marxian dynamics were more descriptive than mathematical. With the rise in interest in simple capital theory problems came the work of such men as Böhm-Bawerk and Wicksell. Again economics was turning away from a world where the effects of changes were seen only through the quantum jumps of comparative statics. Later Harrod and Domar, Solow and Swan, and followers were to develop the dynamics of growth theory with the mathematical exactness characteristic of the neoclassicists. But before this development even began, a young mathematician named Frank Ramsey, writing in 1928, put forth a pioneering solution to the problem, How much of its income should a nation save? In his article, a work perhaps thirty years ahead of its time, Ramsey introduced into economics a method, which had been known to mathematicians for nearly two centuries, for solving a broad range of dynamic optimization problems. The method was known then and now by the name calculus of variations.

The difference between the static and dynamic solution to a maximization or minimization problem is well known. In the former we obtain a single scalar or vectoral solution that holds only at one point or only during one period of time—for example, what baskets of goods to buy, how much to invest, or which game theory strategy to select. In a dynamic problem, the solution takes the form of finding a function, or path, showing the relation between time (the known independent variable) and the quantity representing whatever it is that is to be optimized—for example, the purchase of consumption goods, the amount to be invested, the choice of a game theory strategy.

It is through solving dynamic or over time problems that economists are generally most familiar with optimal path-finding techniques, if indeed they have been introduced at all to these methods. If it is within the purview of economists to find the optimal plots of time versus investment, time versus consumption, and time versus anything else, this placing of time on the horizontal axis of a Cartesian coordinate system is less persistent in the field of pure mathematics. In fact, the seminal problems, which puzzled mathematicians before the time of Euler and which Euler solved formally by development and use of the calculus of variations, did not involve time at all. Rather, they asked for the optimizing curve in the two dimensional space of the physical Cartesian plane.

Like that of the mathematicians, the problem addressed in this book is to find an optimal plane curve in two dimensional geographic space. It should not be hard to appreciate, however, that so long as the problems are intrinsically similar, the mathematical techniques for finding an optimal path are the same regardless of whether the axes are labeled time versus investment, or miles in the abscissa direction versus miles in the ordinate direction, or even apples versus oranges. And so the connection between what will be a spatial optimization problem in this book and the temporal or dynamic optimization problems with so long a history in economics should not be forgotten. Both seek the same objective—an optimal path.

To be specific, the work here deals with radial (also called suburban or urban-suburban) commuter rail lines—that is, rail lines which start at the central business district (CBD) of a city and end somewhere in the suburbs. We address the simple question, Where is it best to locate a suburban rail line? This asks not only for the location of the point where the line[1] ends but also for the path the line takes between the CBD and this endpoint. While we answer these questions for a single rail line, the methods developed may be used to locate more than one line, as pointed out at the end of Chapter 5. A few examples of radial rail lines are shown in Figure 1–1, in which the CBD is taken to be the origin, or (0,0) point.

At the present time there exists no real methodology for solving this problem. With the growth of metropolitan areas in the United States, in other industrialized nations, as well as in the less developed countries,

---

[1] "Line" is used throughout the book to mean "suburban rail line" and has no implication of straightness or linearity attached to it.

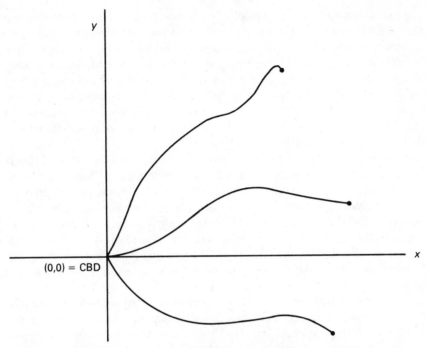

Figure 1–1. Suburban or Radial Rail Lines.

more and more interest has focused on urban rail transport as a means for helping to alleviate congestion and air pollution and more recently to reduce the use of petroleum—as well as to provide users with a rapid form of transportation.[2] While interest in more rail transport has intensified, planning methodologies for locating the lines have not really advanced beyond the simple comparator technique. Here, a small finite number of radial rail line candidates are drawn up and compared on a (usually rather simple) benefit-cost basis. It is unfortunate that when spending hundreds of millions or even billions of dollars to construct a rail system,[3] which may last as long as fifty years, remaining in the same location as originally put, that the rail planners do not have a more powerful planning technique with which to determine line location. Clearly it is desirable to choose the optimal rail line (or optimal rail system—if we construct more than one line) strictly out of basic data on preferences, costs, and so forth—without the awkwardness and limitations of guesswork.

[2] As we shall see in the next chapter, there are many more benefits to building a rail line than this popularized list.

[3] The proposed Washington, D.C., Metro System, with one hundred miles of track divided into eight radial arms, has an estimated construction cost of over five billion dollars.

In addition to this "guesswork" criticism of traditional rail planning techniques, one other fault must be brought forward—namely, that there is often insufficient identification and evaluation of all the costs and benefits of the line. For example, Gannett Fleming Corddry et al. (1974), in their analysis of a proposed two branch extension of the Philadelphia rail system, use a comparator analysis and include only a consideration of revenue, operating costs, and capital costs. While their text mentions a few other costs and benefits, by no means an exhaustive or satisfying list, their calculations include none of these.

Since a knowledge of the costs and benefits of any suburban rail line is a crucial preliminary to being able to determine the best location for the line, Chapter 2 takes up cost-benefit (C-B) considerations. In that chapter, all the costs and benefits of a line are brought forward and discussed. Additionally, various general C-B issues—such as choice of a discount rate, shadow pricing, uncertainty, income distribution, and C-B criteria—are discussed. Results useful to rail planning are summarized, drawing heavily on the modern welfare economics and cost-benefit literature.

Sprinkled throughout this C-B chapter and the remainder of the book are illustrative facts and statistics drawn from the case example of the Lindenwold High Speed Line (HSL). Completed in 1969 and located in the Philadelphia metropolitan area, this radial rail line is a prototypical example of a new breed of intraurban, high speed, modern rail facilities running between the center city and a point in the suburbs. The HLS is the forerunner of the BART system (Bay Area Rapid Transit in San Francisco), the Washington, D.C., Metro, and the proposed lines in Baltimore and Atlanta. It is most appropriate that we use it for purposes of illustration.

Discussing cost-benefit effects and issues is a start toward the ultimate purpose of this book: to provide a sophisticated yet practical tool to planners for the purpose of determining the optimal location of a new radial rail facility. In addition to settling this "where" question, the proposed methodology also settles the "whether" question—namely, whether to build a line at all. This is easily done once the "where" question is resolved—by checking to see if the derived optimal line passes an appropriate C-B test. The choice of appropriate test is discussed in Chapter 2, and the resolution of the "whether" question is discussed further in Chapter 5.

The methodology for solving the optimal rail problem, put simply, runs as follows. List all quantifiable costs and benefits. Derive an explicit mathematical relation that tells how the size of each cost or benefit term varies with the path of the line. Further, derive this relation in such a way that known mathematical techniques can be used to solve for the maximizing path (i.e., the path that maximizes the present discounted value of benefits minus costs; or, in the presence of institutional constraints, some other appropriate benefit-cost expression). This last condition turns out not to be as serious as it might seem, as there exist some extremely robust optimal path-finding methods.

One concept or piece of terminology that it is necessary to understand is the term "functional" (not function—but functional). A "functional" is a mathematical relation that assigns a real number to each function or curve belonging to some class (possibly the class of all functions). The mathematical relations between the geographic path of the rail line (which can be represented in equation form as a curve or function, $y = f(x)$) and the size of a cost or benefit term (a real number) are the functionals we will be dealing with. An example of a simple and well-known functional is the integral from 0 to 1 (for example). This maps from the class of functions that are integrable on the $(0,1)$ interval[4] to the set of real numbers—assigning to each curve the area between it and the x axis—from $x = 0$ to $x = 1$.

The plan for the rest of the book is to discuss cost-benefit considerations in Chapter 2. In Chapter 3 we take up an extensive analysis of rail line demand, using as a case study the Lindenwold HSL. The purpose of this demand analysis is twofold. First, because our optimal rail analysis depends heavily on demand (as will be seen below), it is important to have a mathematical demand equation with worldly relevance—in order that subsequent optimization exercises be realistic. Not only is the form of the equation important, the way line costs are dealt with is also quite significant. Second, with demand playing a crucial and central role, it was felt that a study of the prototypical Lindenwold HSL (hitherto unattempted) would be a very valuable contribution to our knowledge about demand in general.

In Chapters 4 and 5 we take up the optimality procedure itself. Chapter 4 introduces the basic mathematical optimization techniques, while Chapter 5 elaborates on these methods—illustrating further and discussing many of the issues that are likely to confront a rail planner using the optimization methodologies.

The book may be considered then as consisting of three units: cost-benefit analysis (Chapter 2), investigation of demand (Chapter 3), and the optimality procedures per se (Chapters 4 and 5). While the first two units

---

[4] Following traditional mathematical notation, brackets $[a,b]$ will be taken throughout this manuscript to indicate the closed interval from a to b (i.e., all the real numbers from a to b—including the endpoints, a and b), while parentheses (a,b) indicate the open interval from a to b (i.e., all the real numbers from a to b—but not including the endpoints, a and b). A mixture of brackets and parentheses indicates the appropriate half-open, half-closed interval.

feed into the third, all three have been written so that the reader may use them individually and without great need of reading the others.

The level of mathematical sophistication required of the reader is as follows. For Chapters 2 and 3 one needs only an understanding of high school algebra. Chapters 4 and 5 require some comprehension of multivariable calculus.

BIBLIOGRAPHY FOR CHAPTER 1

Gannett Fleming Corddry and Carpenter, Inc., Bellante, Clauss, Miller and Nolan, Inc. 1974. "Summary Report on a Mass Transit Study for the Mass Transportation Development Program of the Delaware River Port Authority." UMTA (project no. IT-09-0009). Xerox.

Ramsey, F.P. 1928. "A Mathematical Theory of Savings." *Economic Journal*, pp. 543–59.

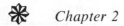 *Chapter 2*

Cost-Benefit Considerations

INTRODUCTION

This chapter provides a summary of all cost-benefit considerations relevant to deciding where it is best to locate a suburban rail line. This is undertaken for two reasons. First,
there has often been insufficient identification and evaluation of rail line
costs and benefits by planners. It is hoped that the rather comprehensive
listing and discussion undertaken here will be of aid to all rail planners,
regardless of whether they utilize the location planning techniques suggested later in this book or older, more informal methods. Second, since a
knowledge of the costs and benefits of a suburban rail line is a crucial
preliminary to being able to determine the best location for the line, this
chapter serves to create a framework for the optimization analysis to
come.

Following this introduction, the chapter is divided into two basic parts.
The first discusses what the costs and benefits of building a suburban rail
line actually are. This part generally also includes mention of who bears
the costs and benefits. This is important if one wants to take distributional
considerations into account.

In this discussion, we divide the costs and benefits into three groups,
based on their general importance and quantifiability—those that are
clearly of great importance and are quantifiable, those that are of uncertain or lesser importance but still are quantifiable, and those that are
generally unquantifiable or very difficult to quantify at the present time.
While only those terms that are quantifiable can be modeled as functionals
and incorporated in the methodology proposed here, after the optimal rail

7

line has been determined on the basis of quantifiable costs and benefits the planner should ask in which direction inclusion of the unquantified terms probably would pull the line. Naturally, he should also ask, Would inclusion of the unquantified terms affect the basic desirability of building the line? It should go without saying that the division of costs and benefits into the three groupings above is a bit sweeping. While the classification may change somewhat in particular applications, we do believe it to be fairly robust.

The second part of the chapter discusses all other considerations needed to write down the cost-benefit expression. After learning who is benefited or harmed and in what way (first part of chapter), the planner must also consider such things as the appropriate discount rate, shadow pricing, length of project life, issues of uncertainty and income distribution, and choice of the appropriate cost-benefit criterion. These and other issues are discussed in this second part of the chapter.

THE COSTS AND BENEFITS OF
A SUBURBAN RAIL LINE

We now turn to the costs and benefits per se, dividing them into three groups, as noted above.

Important and Measurable
Benefits and Costs
Net Revenue of the Line.   Net revenue is the surplus of operating revenues over operating and capital costs. Generally it is negative for suburban rail lines. Its value is easily measurable in money terms, and generally the term is quite significant. The incidence of this benefit or cost is on the taxpayers and receivers of public services[1] if the line is publicly owned. If the line is privately owned, this gain or loss would fall to the owners of the operating company.

It is convenient at this point to also mention the need to include the terminal value of the line at the end of the project evaluation horizon—in addition to revenue and costs. We might also try to consider any dead-

---

[1] The exact group of people affected depends on the method of financing losses or distributing gains. If losses are financed by increasing taxes, or gains distributed by reducing taxes, then the affected group consists of those whose taxes are altered. On the other hand, if losses are financed out of existing tax collections by reducing expenditures on other projects or gains distributed by increasing expenditures on other projects, then the affected group consists of those whose public services are altered. A combination of tax and spending changes is also possible, as is shifting the burden of payment through time (to another "generation" of taxpayers) via debt issue. The inflationary finance method of money creation is also available in the case where some of the costs are paid by the federal government.

weight economic losses from taxation attributable to the construction and operation of the line. However, these excess burdens are usually a very small fraction of total tax yield[2] and hence are probably not worth bothering about.

User Benefits. It is useful to distinguish three classes of users— diverted, generated, and long-run users, the last category often being assimilated into the second in other writings. The distinction between the two made here is that while both groups are undertaking new trips, long-run users have changed home and/or job locations and are undertaking "long-run trips" to or from their new home or job location. All other new trips are considered generated. This distinction is made because benefit measurement to the two groups may be done somewhat differently, as is discussed below. The exact definitions and benefits associated with each group are as follows.

Diverted users make the same trip (i.e., same origin and destination), but use the line instead of their former mode. This group often accounts for a large percentage of total trips, especially in the early years of a new line's operations. A survey[3] of Philadelphia's Lindenwold High Speed Line (HSL) taken nine months after the line's opening revealed that 87.6 percent of the riders were commuters, hence, probably diverted users by and large. In addition, some of the remaining 12.4 percent of users (using the line for shopping, school, recreation, and other purposes) may also have been diverted.

Diverted users include former auto, bus, and train users, as well as those who use empirically less important modes such as motorcycles and bicycles. There may be several dimensions of difference between their formerly preferred mode and the line. These include differences in: (1) cost; (2) expected time of travel (which can be further broken into differences in walking, waiting, and in-vehicle time, as these are generally valued differently by the rider); (3) variance of travel time;[4] (4) comfort (e.g., seat versus no seat, amount of pushing, whether one has to drive or

---

[2] Harberger (1964) computes the deadweight loss of income taxes to be about 2 percent of yield, while Harberger (1966) finds that 3 percent of yield is about the right figure for capital taxes.

[3] See American Automobile Association (1971: 7).

[4] An extreme case that illustrates the importance of this is the deadline example—given by Harrison and Quarmby (1969). Here the rider must be at a certain location by a certain deadline; he is allowed to miss this deadline with a probability that is effectively zero (e.g., he can be late only in case of an earthquake). In this case he must allow the maximum conceivable journey time, however rare it is that this amount of time is taken. In such a case, a reduction of the variability of the journey time (even without any reduction in expected travel time) is a benefit to the consumer in an amount that is equal to the full reduction in the variability. It is easy to see that riders with less rigid schedules would also benefit from a variability reduction, but in lesser degree.

not); (5) aesthetics (what is seen in the vehicle and on the trip; what is heard—loud noises, etc.; what is smelled—noxious odors, etc.); (6) safety; and so forth.

The question is, What is the consumer willing to pay for the package of services embodied in the line, net of what he must actually give up in order to use the line? This is the extra amount the consumer would just be willing to pay if he were made an all-or-nothing offer on whether he could use the line or not.

One way of measuring these diverted user benefits is to try to find the dollar value such riders put on various dimensions of service. This method, if looking at a former bus rider who now rides the line, would look at the fare differentials (crediting any fare saving as a benefit of the line), the value of time differentials, the value of any change in the probability of getting a seat (the study of Foster and Beesley [1963] actually measured this for some users), the value of aesthetic changes, and so on down the list given above.

As it has been employed in the past, one usually did not go any farther than measuring fare and time differentials, and so this method has been an incomplete one for calculating user benefits. However, as we shall see in Chapter 3, there is a good and very workable technique one can use to value the other, more abstract differences between modes.

A traditional method for measuring user benefits is to estimate a demand function, derive its associated demand curve (a plot of price versus quantity—holding all other factors constant), and measure the consumer surplus area under the demand curve.[5] The required demand function is obtained either from survey data on the target population or by using a demand function from a population similar to the target population in tastes, in the service characteristics of the line they use, and in any other characteristics uncontrolled for in the demand function. A fuller discussion of these points is found in Chapter 3.

A third technique for measuring user benefits, employed by the Roskill

---

[5] If the empirically fitted demand curve were at the individual level, we might consider using the area under the compensated or constant utility demand curve, rather than that under the ordinary demand curve. This is the technically correct procedure, as is recognized in Friedman (1949) and even before that in a series of articles by Hicks. However, as Mishan (1971a) points out, the error of this approximation is usually well within the error of statistical (or other) estimation of the demand relation. This is particularly true if, as is often the case, we must extrapolate on the demand curve to prices well above those on which we have actual data—in order to measure surplus. Since the bulk of the triangular surplus area comes from the high price–low quantity part of the curve, which may be only an extrapolation, Mishan's observation takes on added force.

The demand curves used in this book are all based on aggregate, rather than individual, data. In this case, the area under the ordinary demand curve is always used to indicate the surplus benefits, though one must suppose that use of some sort of aggregate of compensated curves might still be a theoretical possibility.

Commission in their study of the third London airport, is to take a survey. Here one would ask people directly how much extra they'd pay in order to be able to use the line, rather than give up rights to make trips on it.

Regardless of which measurement method is used, one must always remember to compare the former mode with the line on the whole trip, in order to deduce diverted user benefits. It is insufficient to compare the two modes only on the part of the trip from the access to the egress station of the line. The line might compare quite favorably on this part of the journey, but if the line user has to make an inconvenient subway or bus connection to reach the end of his trip, then the total rail trip package might not be much of an improvement over his former mode.

Note also that a person may be a diverted user on one trip and a generated user, say, on the next trip; it is not important whether a person falls into more than one category, so as long as his or her trips are properly classified.

Generated users use the line to make trips they didn't used to make—but not to or from a new home or job location. Examples of generated use are seeing (more) shows downtown, going shopping more, seeing friends more, or just going to a different locale for these activities.[6] In advanced countries, where there is already a highly developed transportation network, generated trips from new lines are usually not a very great percentage of total trips. The previously mentioned survey of the Lindenwold HSL seems to put, for the Philadelphia case, an outer limit of about 12 percent on the share of generated users at the time of the survey.

Generated users did not find it worthwhile to make trips from their present origins to their destinations before the line was built. The maximum benefit, therefore, to these users is the difference in fare costs, plus the value of the time differentials, safety differentials, comfort differentials, and so forth, of the line versus the next best mode. This maximum benefit is attained by those generated users who were almost willing to make their trip on the next best mode—and would have, had the cost been reduced by any positive amount. The minimum benefit generated users can be receiving is zero—for those who are just willing to make their generated trips via the line. If one makes the standard assumption that benefits are distributed uniformly from the maximum benefit down to zero, then the average benefit for each generated trip is half the maximum benefit of that trip.

Probably the best way to measure the maximum benefit is to aggregate the value of the cost, time, safety, and other differentials of the line trip

---

[6] Hence, generated users also include those who, for example, go to a different shopping center than they used to after the line is built. The point here is that it does not matter what these users formerly spent their money on, including trips to other places.

versus the trip by the next best mode for the generated trips under consideration. Of course, one does this comparison for the whole trip, as discussed above. Taking half of the maximum benefit so measured yields estimated actual benefits. The problem in the past with using this method is that investigators ran into difficulties measuring much beyond fare and time differentials. However, we may apply the per trip value of the other modal service characteristic differences, as derived for diverted users (by the method to be discussed in Chapter 3), in order to complete the measurement.

We might also try to measure user benefits directly, instead of by finding the maximum benefit and taking half. As for diverted users, ways to do this include taking a willingness-to-pay survey and computing consumer surplus on the basis of an estimated demand function. As for the latter method, it is an unfortunate fact of life that the data needed to estimate a good generated trip demand function are not very often available.

Long-run users have changed their job and/or home locations and use the line to make trips they didn't used to make, to or from their new home or job location. Hence, this includes commuters whose new home and/or job location allows them to use the line. It also includes the noncommutation trips to or from the new home (or job) location.

These long-run users include those who purposely change their home to live near the line (witness the tremendous growth of the town of Lindenwold at the end of the Lindenwold HSL), as well as those who alter their job location to take advantage of line commuting. It also includes those who move into the area around the line and are incidental riders whose main reason for relocating is other than taking advantage of the line's facilities.

The share of riders in this group is generally small in the opening years of a line's operations since the decision to change home or job locations is often a large, long-term one. As time passes, this category becomes more important, its ultimate size depending on population and employment patterns, growth in the region, the cost and attractiveness of alternative trips, and so forth.

The maximum and minimum benefits for these users are just the same as for generated users—obtained by comparing the line to the next best mode for the total trip made. In fact, the three techniques used to measure generated user benefits may be employed here, with just one change. This change applies to the first method, which infers actual benefits as being one half of maximum possible benefits. In the class of long-run users, there are many who move to a new home and/or job location purposely to use the line, and for such people, the actual benefits are likely to be nearer the maximum than the minimum limit. Of course, for those who move into the line's passenger shed with purposes other than use of the line, the distribution of benefits between maximum and minimum is likely to be fairly uniform, as it was with the generated users. The aggregate result is that benefits to long-run users may average more than half the maximum benefit.

A Distributional Epilog. Under certain assumptions (see Polinsky and Shavell [1976] for details), the user benefits of the line, as well as the user disbenefits surrounding modal abandonment (discussed in the next subsection) and neighborhood effects, such as reduced congestion, will be fully capitalized in the value of land and property in the area around the line. If this occurs, then only those who own property in the area will realize these benefits. For example, apartment renters in the line area will find that while getting to work may be cheaper, their rent increases offset these gains. While the line provides gains, they are transferred to the landlords. Homeowners, on the other hand, will find that they can sell their homes for the capitalized value of the benefits, or they can keep them and enjoy the stream of gains. Like the renters, long-run users who come into the area after this capitalization process is complete will find that any gains that the line might have provided to them are taken by whomever provides them a house or apartment.

It was stated above that certain assumptions are needed to guarantee the full capitalization result. One very important assumption, which is not likely to be completely satisfied, is that residential mobility is costless. Because this is clearly not true, it can be shown that full capitalization need not occur. In the real world of costly mobility, the gains (or losses) may be retained, at least partly, by the direct beneficiaries, rather than by the property owners. As the models needed to give guidance on this question are still in the process of being formulated and empirically tested, we cannot be more definite in saying who are the ultimate beneficiaries.

Adjustments in Competing Services. When the line goes into operation, competing transport services may be reduced. For example, buses running routes parallel to the line may be eliminated. Other, less directly competitive, routes may also be closed down if there is sufficient diversion of patronage so as to make them unprofitable to operate. Such adjustments cause losses to those who would still prefer to use the abandoned services.

A loss is clearly indicated when a transport service is eliminated because of the operation of the line, and the displaced riders switch to a nonline mode that was previously available to them. Displaced passengers may also use the line.

Let us consider the second case first. Suppose a bus user switches to the line—after the line goes into operation and his old bus is eliminated. To determine whether or not this person is better off we need only compare the price, time, comfort, safety, and other characteristics of his now nonexistent bus trip with use of the line. We may do this by any of the three techniques discussed under user benefits, above. The important point is that modes eliminated because of the operation of the line must be preserved in the analysis of user benefits. Specifically, if an empirically derived demand curve is used, one must be sure to enter the costs of competing services as they are without the line. Survey methods must set up the questions so that it is clear that competitive facilities are not eliminated. Techniques measuring fare, time cost, and other differentials between the line and the next best mode must allow that next best mode to possibly be one that is or will be closed on account of the construction or operation of the line. User benefit measures that do not consider eliminated transport services will produce overestimates of the welfare of line users. Analysis of a bus user grudgingly forced to the line after his bus route has been eliminated may erringly show a large user benefit if his old favored route is not considered and the next best alternative after the line is highly undesirable.

In addition to the above line user considerations, one must measure the loss to consumers of having to switch from an abandoned mode (e.g., bus or rail) to a mode that is not the line (e.g., private car). As mentioned earlier, this must always represent a loss to the rider so long as the nonline mode was available when the abandoned mode was operating. Also to be measured are the social effects of this mode change—on congestion, land use, payroll benefits, wear and tear on roadways, and many other items, most of which are mentioned in this chapter as costs and benefits of building a line.[7] In addition to considering all these effects for users who switch from an abandoned to a nonline mode, we must also add in the consumer losses (and societal costs and benefits) of those who stop making some of their trips altogether.

In some cases, the costs and benefits of users of an abandoned service switching to a nonline mode or eliminating trips will be so small that they can be essentially ignored. This will occur when there are few riders using the facility even before the line is built or when most or all abandoned users are diverted to the line. In both instances, only a few abandoned service users are not absorbed by the line. The second case, of a high

----

[7] The list of effects to be considered in the case of rail line abandonment is, of course, the same as the list one considers when looking at rail line construction. The two problems are just duals; costs in one case are benefits in the other. And bus line (or other mass transit service) abandonment will have many features in common with rail closures.

percentage of line absorption, will be greatly aided by a network of feeder buses to collect mass transit riders and a good downtown distribution system to get riders to their destinations cheaply and easily.

Reduction in Street Congestion. This generally very significant benefit results from the use of the line by auto and bus riders and the consequent reduction in street traffic. Diverted riders come to mind first when thinking of alleviating congestion, and they are indeed probably most responsible for any decrease in congestion that occurs. However, it is also possible for generated and long-run users, who are making trips they wouldn't have made in the absence of the line, to help lessen congestion. This occurs when new line trips in some sense replace old auto trips. Examples are generated or long-run users who replace a car trip to a shopping center with a line trip to a different shopping center. Replacement of bus and auto trips by line journeys need not be restricted to cases where the trips serve similar purposes. It may also occur through operation of a budget constraint. The line may generate travel. But in order to purchase the line trips, other goods must be given up, among which may be bus or auto trips.

The gains from decongestion are many:

1. Reduction in expected time of travel.
2. Reduction in variance of trip time. (The instability of traffic flow generally lessens as road congestion is mitigated, reducing the variability in travel time.)
3. Reduction in vehicle operating costs. The main items here are[8] a savings in the costs of fuel, maintenance, and repair. These savings are offset somewhat by extra expenditures on tires. In general, the savings from the first items exceed the loss from the increased tire expenditures, resulting in an overall net savings.[9]
4. Reduced nervous strain in driving and riding.

In addition, there may be some change in the incidence and seriousness of (1) injury and death to motorists and pedestrians and of (2) property damage. It seems as though the incidence of accidents causing injury and property damage should decline as the streets become less congested.[10] However, the seriousness of these events may be augmented as a result of

---

[8] See Abelson (1973) for more details.

[9] We are tacitly assuming that rush hour operating speeds are fairly low. At sufficiently high velocities (generally around thirty-five miles per hour or more), further increases in speed will result in greater per mile costs of fuel, maintenance, and repair, as well as tires.

[10] Some studies support this, others find little correlation, still others find a "w" shaped relation between the number of accidents per driven mile and speed—see Steenbrink (1974: 213).

the increased speeds. Hence, there are conflicting directions of influence. The absence of good evidence on the effect of fewer vehicles (operating at higher speeds) on damage, injury, and death rates would seem at this time to preclude measurement of these terms. Even if the effects on injury and death rates were known, these changes would be hard to quantify in money terms.[11]

Also difficult to quantify is reduced nervous strain. Reduced time variance also presents problems, but may not prove intractable with the help of traffic flow studies to derive the reduction in variability and the use of a frequency function showing the distribution of equivalent time gain due to these variability reductions. Reductions in expected travel time and in vehicle operating costs are the easiest to value, and this is done in the Foster and Beesley (1963) study of the Victoria Line in London. These time and money benefits are further discussed in Chapter 5.

The value of all effects could be measured simultaneously if there were data showing how much consumers were willing to pay to drive in less congested traffic conditions. Good data of this sort are unlikely to be available, and the item-by-item approach discussed above is recommended.

Two general notes of caution are sounded with respect to measuring congestion and other benefits. First, after motorists have been attracted to the line and the cost of auto use declines, a certain number of new auto trips will be generated. This mitigates some of the decongestion effects of the line, reducing these benefits.[12] However, the user benefits from these newly generated auto trips will at least partly offset this loss. Second, as decreases in congestion occur, some line users may switch back to using their autos. This effect must be dealt with when predicting line passenger volume.

Land Use Effects.   Suburban rail lines can be a powerful force for promoting development in desired locations and ways. Some line locations will encourage this desired development, while others will help achieve the opposite effect. A judgment concerning the merits of the effects of a given set of links on regional development can only be made with reference to the wants of the region, as often reflected in its development plan.

In some cities, for example, one would attach costs to lines that go "too far" out into the suburbs, since socially undesirable fringe develop-

[11] However, see Mishan (1971b) for a conceptual method of valuing these changes.

[12] Some have even voiced the opinion that there is a "reserve army of motorists" who will take to the road at the first sign of any small reduction in congestion and thus nullify any decongestion gains. See, for example, the discussion of the paper by Foster and Beesley [1963: 85], where this viewpoint is put forth. It is disavowed by some of the other discussants.

ment would then be promoted. Valuing these costs could only be done by recourse to a political process in which area residents, informed of the issues, assess damages or by having local planners who can estimate what the outcome of this process would be.

Land use goals also include the preservation of certain areas as recreational or aesthetic sites. For example, putting the line through a quiet wooded district used for hiking, camping, or just quiet reflection imposes a cost on all those who enjoy these activities in the area and who don't have an equally good alternative. There are many other outdoor activities that may be disrupted by a rail line (see Roskill Commission [1970: 355]). Measurement of the value of recreational (or aesthetic) sites, including those for which no admission fee is charged, is usually accomplished by the use of data on the cost of accessing such sites, together with other information (see, for example, Mansfield [1971] and Roskill Commission [1970: 27–28, 413–25]).

It is convenient to mention at this point the problem of preserving special historic, scientific, or religious sites. Unless these sites are large in a spatial sense, it is generally no problem to leave them intact, merely by moving a part of the line a few hundred yards to one side or the other. Given measurement and other errors in the rest of the cost-benefit analysis and hence in the optimized rail line, this "fine tuning" is probably of little consequence. However, if this is not held to be the case, then these special sites may be incorporated into the analysis much as is done for recreational sites.

The sight and sound of the rail line may disrupt much in addition to recreational activities and special sites. The use of schools, hospitals, libraries, museums, and other public service buildings may be impaired by the noise of the line. Private industry and commerce may be similarly affected. And residential areas may suffer from the noise created by the line as well as from the sight of it. (Although what may be unsightly for some provides a spectator's leisure activity for others, in the form of watching trains.) See Roskill Commission (1970: chs. 18–21, 23, 24) for a measurement methodology one might use in these cases.

It should be borne in mind that in addition to the nuisances associated with operation of the line, there are similar costs stemming from its construction. These include the associated noise, the dust that is raised, the detours that become necessary, and so forth, and may hinder all or any of the above activities. Counterbalancing these costs of construction and operation, more or less, is the decreased noise costs of cars and buses, as users of these modes are attracted to the line.

Loss of Owners' Surplus.   If any homes are taken in order to clear a way for the line, and people are paid market value (plus moving expenses) for their holdings, then there is likely to be a loss in consumer surplus. This will be the case if there are many homeowners who have strong psychological or emotional attachments to their homes, their neighborhood, or the people of the area. In such a situation, mere financial recompense paid at market value does not make up for losses incurred.[13]

Determination of the loss of homeowner surplus can be accomplished by taking a survey that asks people essentially how much would be required to compensate them for having to move. This approach was taken by the Roskill Commission. (The question, as actually phrased in their survey, is criticized by Mishan [1970].) It also may be possible to use a demand equation for housing and to measure surplus in the usual triangular way.

In addition to the losses suffered by homeowners who are forced to move, there are often losses to the friends and associates of those who are displaced. This occurs when those who are uprooted, for one reason or another (e.g., unavailability of suitably priced, comparable housing in the immediate surroundings), move out of the area. A survey may be a good way to determine the extent of these losses.

Owners of businesses and vacant land whose properties are taken in order to make way for the line may suffer losses of producer's and consumer's surplus, respectively. However, the producer surpluses (accruing to businesses with favorable locations with respect to market outlets, labor supply, or whatever) are manifested as financial returns and therefore are reflected in the market value of the businesses. Hence, they should be part of the financial compensation paid. Any consumer surpluses (accruing to owners of vacant land) do not seem so important for nonhomeowners as they are in the case of homeowners. In short, it seems safe to assume that these producer and consumer surplus costs will be small.

Measurable Benefits and Costs of Uncertain or Lesser Importance

Option Value.[14]   We have already discussed measurement of the benefits accruing to those who become users of the line. However, none of

---

[13] Note, however, that if homeowners are not especially attached to an area and would move if some of their relocation costs were eliminated, then paying them market value plus moving expenses can overcompensate them by a sum up to the amount of the moving expense allotment. Generally, however, there is a real aggregate consumer surplus loss to homeowners when they are forced to move. See Roskill Commission (1970: ch. 20), where the amount of such losses incurred by residents around proposed airport sites is discussed.

[14] The seminal article on option value is Weisbrod (1964). Thereafter, the issues raised caused somewhat of a tempest in a teapot. See Long (1967), Lindsay (1969), Cicchetti and Freeman (1971), Schmalensee (1972), Bohm (1975), and Schmalensee (1975)—a series of short articles demonstrating the fun if not the merit of trench warfare.

the techniques mentioned, including the direct approach of asking the users how much extra they would pay rather than forego the privilege of ever using the line, will measure all the option value of the line. There may be people who never use the line yet derive benefit from its existence. Such people have a positive probability of use (e.g., will use the line if their car breaks down), but events have it that they never do in fact become users. These people enjoy what is known as option value.[15] Similarly, line users may derive option value benefits if there are circumstances that would lead them to increase their use.

Option value to nonusers is, of course, not measured by any of the consumer surplus measuring techniques mentioned above for line users. Option value to users is incorporated into user benefits only by the direct survey method. The other methods merely look at the conditions under which actually executed trips are made and then infer a benefit measure. Hence they omit option value (which refers to trips not undertaken).

It may be possible to measure the size of this option value to users and nonusers by use of a willingness to pay question. It is of some importance to establish the significance of this term, since it is often brought forward as a reason for not abandoning a rail line. It would be interesting to know whether this line of argument carries much weight, both in that application and here.[16]

User Taxes and the Reduced Wear and Tear on Roadways. Larsen (1961) finds that frost action and heavy traffic are the two main causes of the need for asphalt road repairs. To the extent that it is auto and bus users who switch to the line, road maintenance and replacement expenditures will be reduced. However, the amount of such reductions is not to be credited as a benefit of the line.

This is because auto, bus, and other vehicle operators pay various taxes (on fuel, tires, etc.) that are used to cover maintenance costs.[17] In fact, Mills (1972: 205) states that for urban streets and highways, automobile users pay somewhat more than maintenance plus construction costs. It is clear that if Mills' statement is true, there is a loss to future roadway taxpayers (or to whomever receives the benefits of these overpayments) when an auto user is diverted onto the line. For while he

[15] Option value is used here in the somewhat restricted sense of the value of trips that are not undertaken (but that had a positive probability of being undertaken). Other writers on the subject have used the term in different ways, which in fact has been the cause for much of the dispute in the literature.

[16] Note that an upper limit to option value for a single user is the cost of using an alternative mode that offers services that are at least as good as those of the line (e.g., taxicab? limousine?).

[17] And which have been included (properly) as a cost of driving in the calculation of user benefits.

causes *x* dollars in costs, he contributes more than this in taxes. Whether buses pay their way toward roadway costs is another question. For both groups, the losses (or gains) should be quite susceptible to measurement.

Payroll Benefits.   A good rail transport system can have many benefits for those who employ a substantial number of line commuters. Reliable service can reduce tardiness as well as the frequency of early dismissals for inclement weather. These benefits were calculated as being significant for the Washington, D.C., Metro (see Metro Rail Impact Study [1975]). In addition, there is a reduced need for carpooling and staggered work hours, the latter being designed to alleviate street congestion. Both of these make an employee's working hours somewhat inflexible.

Unmeasurable or Very Difficult to Measure Benefits and Costs

There are probably substantial additional benefits to building an urban-suburban rail line that are not really susceptible to measurement at the current time. This unquantifiability is due generally to a lack of data as well as to an inability to assess relationships between key variables. Nevertheless, the planner should be aware of these effects and should ask, as mentioned before, In which direction would inclusion of the unquantified terms probably pull the line? and, Would inclusion of the unquantified terms affect the basic desirability of building the line at all?

Air Pollution.   Diverted, generated, and long-run line users attracted onto a modern electric rail line may help alleviate costs of air pollution. Specifically helped are those who are located in the area where vehicular traffic has been lessened; harmed are those who are located near the line's electric power generating source. The net effect is probably beneficial overall—though this conclusion needs to be verified.

Specifically, one would have to examine the amounts of each type of pollutant emitted with and without the line as well as the circumstances (time, place, etc.) under which the pollutants were released. The costs in human morbidity and mortality as well as property loss and destruction of aesthetics (e.g., smog hiding a pleasant view) must then be assessed.[18]

Benefits Especially Associated with Extending Service to the Poor.   The line is capable of providing cheap, reliable transportation between urban employment centers and outlying districts (or between urban ghettoes and

---

[18] See Ridker (1966) for a good discussion of the difficulties in measuring the costs of air pollution. He points out, among other things, that there are three levels of effects with which one must contend: the immediate impact, the actions taken by some to alleviate these effects, and the consequences for others of these actions.

expanding job opportunities in the suburbs). For some, especially the poor, this may mean that new job opportunities are opened up. Hence, the line may help to ease local unemployment and to facilitate advancement to better work opportunities. Fiscal benefits such as reduced welfare payments and increased tax revenues would then be likely to follow.[19] A further likely benefit would be reduced crime.

Maintenance of a Strong Center City Area.   Three offsetting influences of the line seem relevant to understand this effect. The first is that people are encouraged to move their residences out of the city (or if they're already out, to move further away from it). This is the general effect of an improvement in the urban-suburban transport system. The second influence is that businesses tend to be drawn back into the city, especially in and around the central business district, as this area now benefits from having an expanded labor market upon which to draw. Third, shopping in the city is made easier for those in the line's passenger shed. The outflow of people tends to diminish economic activity in the central city, while the influx of business and the increased ease of shopping tends to increase it. It is therefore unclear, a priori, whether the line helps enhance or reduce the position of the CBD as the economic focal point of the metropolitan area. But what is the importance of this?

Rothenberg (1965: 369–70), as well as others, has argued that certain services are lost as the core of a metropolitan area declines. Only in major cities, says Rothenberg, "is there a scale of population concentration large enough to make possible forms of specialized services—opera companies, museums, zoos, specialty shops—which would not be viable with lesser concentrations." If it is true that building a line would add to the range of activities available in the metropolitan region, one would certainly want to count this as a benefit. Likewise, if this range is curtailed, a cost is incurred.

Effects on Oil Usage (Oil Shadow Pricing).   A modern technology, high speed suburban rail line uses many fewer BTUs of energy per passenger mile than an automobile. But it may be somewhat less efficient than buses on this criterion.[20] Thus, when a line is built, it would seem as though there is much potential for energy saving—provided that a sizeable por-

[19] These tax revenues are the only part of the workers' new wage income that need be counted here. The after-tax, disposable part is a benefit to the rail user and will be manifested in his willingness to pay for line services and hence in the user benefits term. Including it here would be double counting.

[20] Boyce et al. (1975: 1) give the BTUs per passenger mile for the Philadelphia-Lindenwold High Speed Line and competing modes as: Line—3,750, bus—2,380, car—9,360. These are based on observed occupancy ratios in this Southern New Jersey corridor.

tion of the users are former auto users rather than former bus users or people making additional trips.

However, even if most passengers are diverted auto users, it still may be the case that energy use will be higher with the line than without it. This is because use of the line entails in most cases that a more round-about trip be made than if an auto were used instead. And it is frequently the case that the energy-hungry auto is used for part of a rail trip—namely, for access from home to a line station. In fact, Boyce et al. (1975) found that in the case of the Philadelphia-Lindenwold High Speed Line, total energy consumption rose when the line was installed. This is a surprising conclusion, though its force is weakened somewhat by certain measurement problems.

Even if it is the case that the line causes an increase in energy consumption, it may nevertheless permit a substantial drop in oil usage. This will be the case for an electrically powered line where the power is provided by fuels other than oil (e.g., coal or nuclear fuel).

An increase or decrease in oil consumption is to be taken account of in cost-benefit analysis only if one believes that the current market price of oil does not reflect its social optimum price. As this book is being written, the possibility of another OPEC oil embargo still hangs over the Western countries, threatening them with domestic disruptions and with pressures to alter their foreign policy in ways that they would not have otherwise chosen. It is clear, then, that there are substantial externalities associated with the private use of oil and oil products. Whether or not these are fully captured in the present price of oil (already selling at levels substantially above private production costs) or whether prices that would yield a greater amount of autarchy and higher domestic production are desired is what must be decided. And it must be decided at the level of national policymaking—not by local rail planners—for clearly, the shadow price of petroleum is a national parameter, and the same value should be used in project evaluations in other parts of the economy. At this time, it seems as though no coherent energy program has been launched in the United States, and the political process needed to help establish an abstract measure like the shadow price of oil has not yet taken place. Nor have the economists come to any consensus on what the long-run supply costs of energy from alternative sources is. Not long ago this was thought to be $7–9 per barrel of oil replacement, but this figure is surely too low. Short-run supply costs of alternative energy are of course much greater.

Secondary Effects.   Economists have yet to really come to grips with the question of how to deal correctly with secondary effects. These basically refer to Keynesian multiplier effects (both positive and negative) stemming from expenditures and economic activity level changes surrounding the project. They present not only difficulties in correct treatment from a theoretical standpoint, but also entail tremendous measurement problems because of the diversity of effects involved.

Some economists have tried to show that under a certain reasonable set of conditions, secondary effects can be totally dispensed with. Unfortunately, the set of conditions required is, under most circumstances, not very reasonable upon close inspection. Illustrating this, Westley (1976: 71–77), derives one set of sufficient (though not necessary) conditions (given here in summary form) under which secondary effects are nil.

1. There is a part of the federal government that sets and achieves overall macroproduction targets (on the value of aggregate production).
2. The overall income multiplier is the same for the line as for the project(s) it displaces.
3. There are equal divergences between the market and social values of the secondary effects of the line vis-à-vis the project(s) it displaces.

On the other hand, assumptions sufficient to justify full consideration of secondary effects, as if they were primary, are also unpalatable. One such set of assumptions is given by Gittinger (1972: 27):

> (1) the public expenditure is not financed out of tax revenues so that the multiplier-creating expenditures are not drawn away from the private sector: (2) the conditions of supply for all factors stimulated to employment by the investment are perfectly elastic at prevailing prices: (3) the opportunity costs of these factors in the absence of the investment are zero: and (4) the outputs which result do not simply substitute for other products in the market place and thus, do not result in unemployment for other factors of production.

GENERAL COST-BENEFIT CONSIDERATIONS

We now turn to a discussion of traditional cost-benefit principles. This will complete the framework of analysis, allowing one to take all the items in the previous section and form them into a cost-benefit expression. The topics to be discussed in this section are, in order: (1) choice of the appropriate discount rate and the shadow price of investment, (2) other shadow prices, (3) relative and absolute price changes, (4) length of project life and choice of discount date, (5) cost-benefit criteria, (6) uncertainty considerations, and (7) income distribution. The discussions will be kept brief, as they serve only as summaries of what can be found in the cost-benefit literature.

Choice of the Appropriate Discount Rate
and the Shadow Price of Investment

On perhaps no other cost-benefit topic does one find as much confusion as there is concerning the choice of the appropriate discount rate. To begin, let us assume that project benefits consist of consumption created and project costs consist of consumption lost. Then the appropriate discount rate is what is called the social time preference (STP) rate. The STP rate is nothing more than society's valuation of consumption next year relative to consumption this year. If this rate were 6 percent, this would mean that \$1 of consumption today is equally valuable as \$1.06 of consumption next year. This is clearly the correct concept under the above assumption.

But it may well be that at least some of the project costs will be in terms of displaced or foregone investment. And some of the returns from the project may be used directly for investment (and perhaps reinvestment) rather than for immediate consumption. What do we do in these cases?

Suppose that \$1 invested today yields a perpetual stream of \$$q$ per year, q being the marginal productivity of capital. Of these returns, suppose a share, s, is reinvested upon receipt (the remainder, \$$q$ $(1 - s)$, being consumed each year). Then it is easy to show that \$1 of current investment is worth $\frac{(1 - s)\,q}{i - sq}$ dollars of current consumption, where $i =$ the STP rate used for discounting consumption.[21] That is, the shadow price of investment, in terms of a consumption numéraire, is given by $\frac{q - sq}{i - sq}$.[22] One should, then, break down project benefits and costs into consumption and investment components and apply such a markup factor to all investment flows. One then discounts this stream of consumption and consumption equivalents using the STP rate.

While the STP rate could, of course, vary over time, it is invariably treated as a constant. Even as a single parameter, how can it be measured? Let us start back one square.

The time preference rate for an individual (ITP) reflects that individual's relative valuation of consumption at different given times. This rate can, in a world of imperfect capital markets (with, for example, borrowing rates unequal to lending rates, and perhaps more than one rate of each type), differ among individuals. Society, one might reason, being no more

[21] This expression holds so long as $i > sq$, which is extremely likely. If $i < sq$, then the shadow price of investment must be expressed as an infinite sum.

[22] Note that if $i = q$—that is, if the social time preference rate equals the marginal productivity of capital—the shadow price of investment is equal to one. That is, investment and consumption are equally valuable. Generally it is felt that $i < q$, so that the shadow price of investment is greater than one (i.e., investment is more valuable than consumption). However, given the slipperiness of the STP concept, it is difficult to be sure of this.

than a collection of individuals, would then have its STP rate equal to a consumption-weighted average of individual discount rates, these discount rates being equated to market interest rates under the standard Fisherian model.

Several forceful objections to this line of argument have been raised in the literature. While it would take us too far afield to consider these, excellent summaries are contained in Layard (1972) and UNIDO (1972: ch. 13). In a word, the arguments are that interest rates fail to account for the welfare of future generations, certain types of consumption externalities, myopia, and other important considerations. Despite the obstacles, the analyst is still faced with the problem of arriving at an appropriate STP rate.

The most widely employed method is still to use posttax interest rates on long-term (if the project is long term) bonds. However, one major school of cost-benefit thought, most recently championed by Squire and van der Tak (1976), advocates the use of an intertemporal social utility function together with an estimate of the rate of growth of consumption. The idea here is that the faster the rate of growth of the economy, the higher should be the STP rate, since the individual's income will be that much greater in the future, and further consumption will be worth less at the margin. Still, however, some judgment is needed on the rate at which marginal utility declines with increased consumption. Due to the practical limitations on actually finding the correct discount rate, studies often try more than one such number—say, 4 percent, 7 percent, and 10 percent. The sensitivity of project rankings (or, in the case here, rail line location) to the choice would then be examined.

Other Shadow Prices[23]

Because some markets are distorted (for example, by taxes or monopoly) or are in disequilibrium, the price of goods traded in these fora will not always reflect their value. Other types of goods are not subject to economic exchange, and so there exists no market price at all in these cases. Instances of the latter (nonexistent markets) that are relevant to rail planning come up frequently—for example, in the valuation of time saved by users of the line and by motorists driving on decongested streets, of life, of air pollution effects, and of crime reduction. The general guiding principle, here as throughout cost-benefit analysis, is to value beneficial effects at the maximum the beneficiary would be willing to pay rather than forego them and to value deleterious effects at the minimum the recipient would be willing to accept in compensation. Beyond this general principle, the discussion must necessarily devolve into specific instances and special techniques. For example, Chapter 3 of this book uses regression

---

[23] This subsection owes much to the lucid discussion of Layard (1972).

analysis to try to get at the value of time, and Mishan (1971b) attempts to transform the question of the value of life into one of evaluating changes in the probability of death, which he claims is usually a more relevant question anyway. The interested reader is referred to McKean (1968) and Margolis (1977) for further discussion on the valuation of costs and benefits in nonexistent markets.

For the case of distorted or disequilibrated markets, there are also numerous cases to consider. For example, if a purchased material input is subject to indirect taxes or is produced by a monopolist, then the purchase price will in general be above the marginal production cost. Should we use the price or the marginal production cost for purposes of valuation? The answer is that it depends on whether the project's use of this input reduces the amount available to other domestic purchasers or whether there will be an increase in supply. If the good is in fixed supply, then it should be valued at its opportunity cost in other uses, which is given by its market (demand) price. If, on the other hand, total production of the input increases by the full amount used in the project, the correct valuation would be the marginal production cost. For intermediate cases, we use a weighted average of the price and marginal cost.

Labor and foreign exchange have also been the subjects of extensive shadow-pricing discussions. For example, if the project employs construction workers during a time of great unemployment in this sector, it may be giving jobs to those who would have been otherwise totally unemployed. In this case, the cost to the economy of employing these workers may be well below their market wages—even zero under certain circumstances.

If the project requires a substantial amount if imported material, and the country currently has an overvalued currency, being propped up by government intervention and a draining of foreign exchange reserves, then the value of foreign exchange may well be above the official exchange rate. In this case, we should employ a shadow price of foreign exchange.

Both the shadow pricing of labor and of foreign exchange are discussed well in UNIDO (1972), Little and Mirrlees (1974), and Squire and van der Tak (1976). The last two works take a rather inverted (though in some ways easier) approach to foreign exchange shadow pricing since they employ savings in the form of freely convertible foreign exchange as numéraire, in place of consumption.

General Inflation and Relative Price Changes

There is little disagreement on the need to eliminate pure price inflation from the analysis. One way to accomplish this is to use current prices (for goods and services purchased or produced by the project now and in the future) and a nominal discount rate. A more frequently used method is to use constant prices (e.g., the set of prices prevailing at the start of the project, adjusted for any peculiar seasonal or cyclical aspect) and a "real" rate of discount.[24] Both of these methods eliminate pure price inflation. The first, however, automatically allows for relative changes in prices—between the prices used in the project and the general price level. This is, of course, desirable, and to allow for this in the second method is a simple matter. One merely attaches a compounding (or other) trend to the prices that are thought to rise more quickly or slowly than the rest. The size of the trend reflects the differences in the relative rates of growth of the prices.

An example of this is found in the Roskill Commission (1970) report on the third London airport. In that study, a real discount rate of 10 percent is used. Constant prices are employed, except that the price of leisure time is taken to increase at 3 percent per year and the cost of noise nuisance to grow at 5 percent per year—these two trends reflecting the belief that the cost of leisure hours and noise nuisance will rise over time relative to the other prices in the economy.

Length of Project Life and Choice of Discount Date

There is, of course, no way to predict how long a rail line will provide services. Physical deterioration and obsolescence combine to put a finite limit on the length of time over which such a project should be evaluated. Fifty years is a frequently used horizon. Foster and Beesley (1963) use this project life in their analysis of London's Victoria Line. The Washington, D.C., Metro Impact Study (see Metro Rail Impact Study [1975]) uses a horizon of forty-eight years in its calculations. While there is no pat answer to the length of life question, Foster and Beesley (1963: 50) express well the considerations one must deal with in making a choice:

> For this paper it [the length of life of the Victoria Line] is assumed to be 50 years operation. This does not imply a prediction that all capital will need to be replaced by then. The tunnels and earthworks should never need it. But it is rash to assume in this kind of calculation that a capital asset, though it lasts forever, will have value forever: it is always possible that scientific progress or changes in the location of population or industry, etc., will make the Victoria Line obsolete. To guard against obsolescence, it is necessary to limit the period of time over which benefits (and costs) are counted. The choice of period was arbitrary within limits of what seemed reasonable.

[24] That is, allowing prices to rise by a factor of $(1 + p)$ per year and discounting with the factor $(1 + r)$, is the same as keeping prices stable and discounting by the "real" rate $(1 + r)/(1 + p)$. For r and p close to zero, $(1 + r)/(1 + p)$ is nearly equivalent to $(1 + r - p)$. Hence the real discount rate is often taken as $(r - p)$.

The choice of horizon is a parameter, like the discount rate, on which one might choose to perform a sensitivity analysis. It is quite possible to find, as Foster and Beesley did when they tried project lives of ninety years and an infinite span, that the effects in the later years are so heavily discounted that they scarcely affect the calculations.

As for selecting a discount date, the choice of the time to which all costs and benefits should be discounted is arbitrary and makes no difference whatever to the formal analysis. The only point to be made here is that we may want to select one date over another so as to be able to better compare differences in quantified costs and benefits against unmeasured terms. This may call for discounting at least up to a given time at which these unquantified effects begin.

Cost-Benefit Criteria

The fundamental criterion used in cost-benefit analysis for decisions of whether to undertake a project is to do so, so long as it has a positive present discounted value of benefits minus costs. Discounting takes place at the social time preference (STP) rate, discussed earlier. The criterion for selection of the best project from among alternatives is to choose the one that has the highest net present discounted value. If forced to choose just one, we would therefore be choosing the project that adds the most to social welfare.

These two rules work well so long as there are no outside constraints, such as a budget constraint. For they tell us to build a line if we can find a location that yields a positive net benefit, and if there is more than one such location, to choose the one with the greatest net benefit. But suppose there is a budget constraint—say, on the present discounted value of total cash outlays. Then we'd want to choose the project that maximizes $(B - C)/C_1$ where

B = present value of all project benefits
C = present value of all project costs
C_1 = constrained costs (here: the present value of total cash outlays).

In this way, we select the project with the biggest bang (i.e., net return = $B - C$) per buck of constrained cost (i.e., C_1). While this would select for us the best rail project from the set of all possible rail projects, it does not tell us whether or not to build this best line. This decision is made by comparing the best line with projects in other sectors that are under consideration, and ranking all these in order of $(B - C)/C_1$. The rail project is undertaken if it ranks high enough on the list so as to be affordable within the cutoff of the budget constraint. Note that this process is a discrete analogy to the process by which a consumer (with a meaningful cardinal utility function) spends his money under a budget constraint. He buys first the goods that give him maximum marginal utility per dollar spent.

In addition to budget constraints, there may be distributional constraints placed upon the project. These can take diverse forms and would seem to be more politically than economically inspired. One example would be to maximize overall net present value subject to the constraint that certain groups obtain at least a minimum of net benefits from the project. These groups might be selected on the basis of income, geographical location, and so forth. While equity is certainly at issue here, it would seem to be a better idea to weight the benefits and costs to different groups differently (marking up the effects on favored groups heavily) and then find the line that maximizes the present value of these weighted net benefits.

Uncertainty Considerations

There is uncertainty about the magnitude of all costs and benefits listed in this chapter. For example, it is not certain what the costs and revenues of the line will be, and so the amount of taxpayer subsidy (or return) is not known for sure. However, as Arrow and Lind (1970) point out, when the dollar amount of the uncertainty is spread over enough taxpayers, or other agents, the risk may be so small for each of them that it can be ignored.

For example, an expenditure of $5 billion (the estimated construction cost of the Washington, D.C., Metro) plus or minus $3 billion say—all of which is borne by the federal government and thus spread over seventy-five million taxpayers—involves an average risk of ±$40 per person. For most people, the prospect of having their taxes raised or lowered $40 is not economically very significant. They would probably value say a fifty-fifty chance of gaining or losing $40 at about the expected value of zero. Some people might enjoy the gamble and others might be mildly opposed. The insignificance of the risk is probably even more convincing if the gain or loss of $40 is broken up into a series of payments over many years—as would occur if the government debt financed the line.

If it is true that the effects on the ultimate risk bearers is negligible, then we need not assign any risk penalty in the form of costs exceeding their expected value or benefits being below their expected value. While it cannot be argued a priori that the construction costs of every line project will involve negligible risk for the taxpayers, who customarily pay for these expenses nowadays, it seems to this author that this will be true for all but the hugest of rail undertakings. And even in this case, it is only the uncertainty about the size of the state and local shares (which are 20 percent) of construction costs that are likely to have any serious risk implications for taxpayers (due to the substantially smaller number of them at the local level).

The variance in operating deficits (revenue minus operating costs) is generally small compared to that of capital expenditures, and the taxpayer risk here is a fortiori negligible. But what about farepayer risk? Suppose the average fare is 50¢. (It was actually less for the Philadelphia-Lindenwold Line—see American Automobile Association [1971].) Also, suppose there is a fifty-fifty chance that fares will be adjusted upward or downward by 20 percent—say, to correctly reflect marginal social costs or, as in the case of the London Transport System, to cover expenses and break even. This means a 10¢ per ride risk. For the faithful commuter, using the line twice a day, five days a week, and fifty weeks per year, the risk is $\pm(10$¢/ride$)$ $(500$ rides$)$ $= \pm$\$50 per year. This is 1 percent of an after-tax income of \$5,000, an income number that is well below the national average. Again, it seems as though the risk is not great—at least within the range of a 20 percent adjustment on a 50¢ fare.

Having looked briefly on the cost side at two major groups, the taxpayers and farepayers, who bear costs of the line, we turn to some of the beneficiaries of the line. As for the users of the facilities, there is risk that the line won't run on a particular day or will derail, catch fire, or otherwise not provide normal service. All these factors affect people's willingness to pay for line services—and hence affect user benefits. Therefore if we can measure user benefits accurately, we will already have a measure that reflects the disutility of these risks. People will have revealed the certain sum of money they are willing to exchange for an uncertain package of services. No further consideration or risk is warranted here.

Many of the other benefits detailed earlier in this chapter depend on the number of riders the line garners. They may also depend on whether the line trip is replacing a former trip, the previous mode, the length of the trip, the origin and destination, and on other factors. For example, a reduction in street congestion and air pollution depends on attracting many auto users to the line, especially those making long trips in well-traveled corridors at rush hours. Reducing oil use and wear and tear on roadways also depends on these factors, though perhaps more strongly on the number of auto miles eliminated and less forcefully on the exact location and timing of the excised trips.

In addition to pointing out some sources of uncertainty for these four benefits (because of our imperfect ability to make forecasts about what kind of users will be attracted to the line, etc.), the above has shown that there is most certainly not independence among these different terms. If, for example, the number of riders the line garners is below the expected figure, then congestion, pollution, oil saving, and road maintenance saving benefits will all, it is likely, be reduced. This means that we must consider several nonindependent risks impinging on many of the parties affected by the line. The potentially cumulative nature of such risks must be considered.

Despite this nonindependence, there still may be a case for maintaining that the risks to most of the ultimately affected parties are small relative to their income. A good study on congestion benefits is Foster and Beesley (1963: 70), which finds that traffic in the area where congestion would be alleviated by the Victoria Line speeds up about 5 percent or roughly 0.5 miles per hour. While this yields large aggregate gains, the size of benefits and the uncertainty concerning this size are not very large for any individual. An individual would save about three minutes on a one hour trip. Commuting an above average two hours per day or five hundred hours per year, this amounts to a saving of about twenty-five hours in the year. Multiplying this by a recent figure on the value of line haul time savings (see Merewitz et al. [1975a]) of $3 per hour, we get a saving of $75 per year for a long distance, regular auto-using commuter. While forecasting rail traffic is a risky art, the uncertainty attached to a gain of $75 per year, in terms of a likely range, is probably less than ±$75.

Now we must aggregate with this the risk concerning the pollution, oil saving, and other similar gains of the line project—taking due account of the statistical dependencies and independencies of the effects. It is unfortunate that there is little more usable data extant that would help us decide on the size of the individual benefits per person involved in a typical rail project. Even being able to do this in the simplistic fashion employed here enables one to get a useful feel for the general size of the risks. So far, they do not seem overly large. Of course the size and other particulars of the given rail project under study at the time will ultimately bear upon the decision of whether or not to make any special allowance for risky returns.

If there is to be an adjustment for risky returns, there are two main ways to proceed. The first is to reduce the value of uncertain outcomes to a certainty equivalence number. This involves ascertaining the cost of risk, which necessitates employing a utility function. This is illustrated in Figure 2–1. Suppose a risk averter with a utility of income function shown by WW has a fifty-fifty lottery chance of receiving either y or $3y$. His expected utility is $(1/2)U(y) + (1/2)U(3y)$. The certain amount of money required to yield this same amount of utility is c, while the expected value of the lottery is $2y$. The cost of risk is $(2y - c)$ dollars. Having now obtained a certainty equivalence of c for the risky returns, one need only discount at the riskless rate should the gains occur in the future.

The second method for accounting for risks is to use a higher than certainty rate to discount any benefits of the project. Conversely risky costs should be discounted with a lower than certainty rate, so as to mark

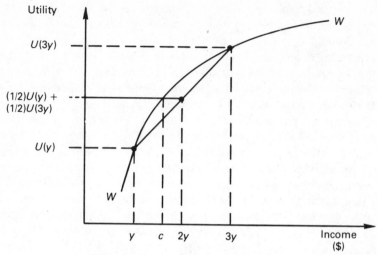

Figure 2–1. The Cost of Risk.

them up. The degree of divergence between the discount and the riskless rate will increase as the risk does. As Prest and Turvey (1965) point out that this method is strictly appropriate only where uncertainty compounds over time.

Income Distribution

Welfare economics divides the [policy] question into two analytically separate parts: (1) is the program "efficient," and (2) are the income-redistribution effects (if any) "desirable"? For reasons that will be discussed shortly, advice given by economists to decision makers tends to be restricted to questions of the first type. At the same time, actual decisions do, and should, also reflect answers to questions of the second type. As a result, economists are often disappointed that their advice carries little weight. . . .[25]

One of the criticisms Mishan (1970) and many others had of the Roskill Commission cost-benefit study on the siting of the third London airport was that it failed to incorporate income distribution effects into the analysis. While the distributional effects were shown in a separate table in the report, they were not embedded in the actual cost-benefit calculations and hence did not affect the ranking of the sites. Mishan also raised the prospect that the big beneficiaries of a third London airport may be the

[25] B.A. Weisbrod (1968: 171).

"business tycoons and the Mallorca holiday-makers," in which case the economic justification for building the airport at all may be undermined.

So it is with rail lines. Choice of distributional weights can powerfully affect where the optimal line is located. Heavily weighting benefits to low income areas can push the line in that direction. It should be pointed out that often suburban rail lines have been located so that the more well to do suburbanites receive most of the benefits, while taxpayers in general (who usually have a lower average income than the rail users) cover the deficits. This results in an income redistribution from the poor to rich, and this perverse effect should be accounted for in the analysis. Frankena (1973) documents this effect for several Canadian transit systems.

In short, I strongly recommend, like Weisbrod, that income distribution effects be built into the cost-benefit analysis and into the rail line location algorithm. A weighting method will be discussed shortly that allows for both of these. In addition, by setting each of the weights equal to 1, a neutral position on income distribution can be taken in which gains to both rich and poor are treated equivalently. This equal weighting would be desirable even from a theoretical point of view if it is felt that income would have been redistributed anyway (by a tax and transfer mechanism, say) even if the line project hadn't been undertaken. In this case, it is not appropriate to differentially weight gains to the various income classes. Rather, we should assign a benefit to the project equal only to the administrative and other cost savings to the agency that would have performed the redistribution. If the agency would have done this with additional efficiency losses (excess burden) these may also be credited to the line.

As Galbraith (1969) points out, for the past several years in the United States the income distribution issue has been politically dormant. It is probably not the case, therefore, that the income redistribution effects of a line are redundant.

If we are to integrate equity and efficiency, it is easiest (following Weisbrod [1968] and others) from an operational point of view to assume a Bergsonian social welfare function which involves additivity over individuals and constant welfare weights. That is:

$$W = w_1 + w_2 + \ldots + w_n \tag{2.1}$$

where W = total welfare of society
$\quad\quad w_i$ = welfare of ith individual
and,

$$dW = a_1(dy_1) + a_2(dy_2) + \ldots + a_n(dy_n) \tag{2.2}$$

where dy_i = change in net benefits (welfare) of ith person, measured in money terms

a_i = welfare weight of ith person, essentially his marginal utility of income (These may all = 1, in which case a neutral or strict efficiency position is taken.)

In more complicated formulations, we could allow for interdependencies of one person's welfare on another's or of decreasing weights for large positive income increments. Other nonlinearities and possibly other variables might also enter. In an operational sense most of these changes are not practical.

Even accepting the simple formulation of equation (2.2), we still have the problem of deriving the a_i weights. There have been several suggestions in the literature, many of which are summarized by Nwaneri (1970). None are above objection, either for being arbitrary and oversimplified or because they contain internal inconsistencies. A few are summarized here.

Foster (1966) suggests $\bar{y}/y_i$ as the weight for all costs and benefits accruing to the ith individual or group. $\bar{y}$ is the mean income of the population and y_i is the income of the ith affected individual or the mean income of the ith affected group. Eckstein (1961) tries to use effective marginal tax rates to derive the government's notion of the relative marginal utility of income to different people. Freeman (1967) has pointed out difficulties with this method, though. Wise et al. (1970) derive weights using the marginal utility of income functions proposed by Frisch (1959) and McGuire and Garn (1969). Finally, Weisbrod (1968) tries to infer an implicit set of distribution weights from government decisions on which of the set of various projects open to it were adopted in the past. But as Layard (1972: 59) points out, "there is an obvious logical objection to this approach: either the government's decisions so far have been consistent, in which case why worry about helping it continue to be consistent, or they have been inconsistent, in which case why pretend they were consistent." These four are some of the main schemes that have been used in the past to derive distributional weights. All of them, except Weisbrod's, assume implicitly that it is desirable to redistribute income from rich to poor. Galbraith (1969) raises the possibility that conservatives may feel that the reverse is desirable, in view of the high tax rates that are (at least nominally) applied to the upper income brackets.

In addition to deciding on the welfare weights we must also break down the costs and benefits listed above and look at the effects on various income groups. For example, if costs exceed revenues and we know certain taxes will be raised to cover the deficit, then we must try to figure out, as best we can, which taxes will be increased and by how much. From this, the effect on people of various incomes is derived.

It will also happen that for certain benefits and costs (one example being user benefits) we will have a natural *geographic* breakdown of the effect. In this case, the practical and suggested procedure is to look at the average income in each geographic district. Then weight benefits and costs to each zone according to the average income there. This has the implicit hope behind it that there is a fair amount of income uniformity within the zone. Census tracts are rather ideal for this purpose, as they are specifically drawn up with uniformity of economic and other characteristics in mind.

Instead of subdividing the costs and benefits into effects on specific income classes or geographic zones, we may just wish to look at the average income of all those in a particular functional group. Thus, we might look at the average income of all those enjoying decongestion benefits, option value, generated trips, and so forth. Distributional calculations then proceed from this level. Categories can even be combined if necessary. This is the most aggregative of the three techniques suggested, but may be useful in the face of practical data or other limitations. The Roskill Commission (1970: 448–49) lumps all affected parties into only four broad groups. In the work on rail lines, it is anticipated that all three distributional techniques might be employed.

BIBLIOGRAPHY FOR CHAPTER 2

Abelson, P.W. 1973. "Quantification of Road User Costs." *Journal of Transport Economics and Policy*, pp. 80–97.

Alder, H.A. 1971. *Economic Appraisal of Transport Projects: A Manual with Case Studies*. Bloomington: Indiana University Press.

American Automobile Association. 1971. *The Lindenwold Line*. Washington, D.C.

Angel, S., and G.M. Hyman. 1971. "Urban Travel Time." *Regional Science Association—Papers and Proceedings (European Conference)*.

Arrow, K.J., and R.C. Lind. 1970. "Uncertainty and the Evaluation of Public Investment Decisions." *American Economic Review*, pp. 364–78.

Baum, H.J. 1973. "Free Public Transport." *Journal of Transport Economics and Policy*, pp. 3–19.

Bohm, P. 1975. "Option Demand and Consumer's Surplus: Comment." *American Economic Review*, pp. 733–36.

Bone, A.J. 1952. "Travel Time and Gasoline Consumption Studies in Boston." *Highway Research Board Proceedings*, pp. 440–56.

Boyce, D.E.; K. Nguyen; T. Noyelle; and V. Vuchic. 1975. "Impact of Rapid Transit on Fuel Consumption and Cost for the Journey to Work." Xerox.

Cicchetti, C., and M. Freeman III. 1971. "Option Demand and Consumer Surplus: Further Comment." *Quarterly Journal of Economics*, pp. 528–39.

Cope, E., and L. Liston. 1961. "A Discussion of Gasoline Tax Rates and Gasoline Consumption." *Highway Research Board Proceedings*, pp. 51–70.

Eckstein, O. 1961. "A Survey of the Theory of Public Expenditure Criteria." In

J.M. Buchanan, ed., *Public Finances: Needs, Sources and Utilization.* Princeton, N.J.: Princeton University Press.

Else, P.K., and M. Howe. 1969. "Cost-Benefit Analysis and the Withdrawal of Railway Services." *Journal of Transport Economics and Policy*, pp. 178–94.

Evans, R.D. 1972. "Fare Revenue and Cost-Benefit Analysis." *Journal of Transport Economics and Policy*, pp. 321–23.

Feldstein, M. 1964. "The Social Time Preference Discount Rate in Cost-Benefit Analysis." *Economic Journal*, pp. 360–79.

———. 1973. "The Inadequacy of Weighted Discount Rates." In R. Layard, ed., *Cost-Benefit Analysis*. Baltimore: Penguin.

Floyd, C., and T. Robertson. 1971–1972. "Some Urban Policy Considerations of Rural Journey-to-Work Commuting." *Review of Regional Studies*, pp. 29–36.

Flowerdew, A. 1972. "Choosing a Site for the Third London Airport: the Roskill Commission's Approach." In R. Layard, ed., *Cost-Benefit Analysis*. Baltimore: Penguin.

Foster, C.D. 1966. "Social Welfare Functions and Cost-Benefit Analysis." In R. Lawrence, ed., *Operational Research and Social Sciences*. London: Tavistock Publishing.

Foster, C.D., and M.E. Beesley. 1963. "Estimating the Social Benefit of Constructing An Underground Railway in London." *Royal Statistical Society Journal*, pp. 46–93.

Frankena, M. 1973. "Income Distributional Effects of Urban Transit Subsidies." *Journal of Transport Economics and Policy*, pp. 215–30.

Freeman, A.M. 1967. "Income Distribution and Planning for Public Investment." *American Economic Review*, pp. 495–508.

Friedman, M. 1949. "The Marshallian Demand Curve." *Journal of Political Economy*, pp. 463–74.

Frisch, R. 1959. "A Complete Scheme for Computing all Direct and Cross Demand Elasticities in a Model with Many Sectors." *Econometrica*, pp. 177–96.

Galbraith, K. 1969. *The Affluent Society*. 2nd ed. New York: Mentor.

Gannett Fleming Corddry and Carpenter, Inc., Bellante, Clauss, Miller and Nolan, Inc. 1974. "Summary Report on a Mass Transit Study for the Mass Transportation Development Program of the Delaware River Port Authority. UMTA (project no. IT-09-0009). Xerox.

Gittinger, J.P. 1972. *Economic Analysis of Agricultural Projects*. Baltimore: Johns Hopkins University Press.

Goering, J. 1971. "Transporting the Unemployed." *Growth and Change*, pp. 34–37.

Grime, G. 1952. "Traffic and Road Safety Research of the Road Research Laboratory, England." *Highway Research Board Proceedings*, pp. 466–86.

Harberger, A.C. 1964. "Taxation, Resource Allocation and Welfare." In *The Role of Direct and Indirect Taxes in the Federal Revenue System*. Conference report of the National Bureau of Economic Research and the Brookings Institution. Princeton, N.J.: Princeton University Press.

———. 1966. "Efficiency Effects of Taxes on Income and Capital." In M. Kryzaniak, ed., *Effects of Corporation Income Tax*. Detroit: Wayne State University Press.

Harrison, A.J., and D.A. Quarmby. 1969. "The Value of Time in Transport Planning: a Review." In *Theoretical and Practical Research on an Estimation of Time-Saving.* European Conference of Ministers of Transports, Report of the Sixth Round Table. Paris: Economic Research Center.

Hirsch, W.Z., and P. Goodman. 1967. "Is There an Optimum Size for a City?" in M. Edel, and J. Rothenberg, eds. 1972. *Readings in Urban Economics.* New York: MacMillan Co.

Hirschleifer, J. 1958. "On the Theory of Optimal Investment Decision." *Journal of Political Economy*, pp. 329–52.

Kain, J.F. 1972. "How to Improve Urban Transportation at Practically No Cost." *Public Policy*, pp. 335–58.

Larsen, M. 1961. "Iowa County Highway Maintenance Programs." *Highway Research Board Proceedings*, pp. 497–511.

Layard, R. 1972. "Introduction." In R. Layard, ed., *Cost-Benefit Analysis.* Baltimore: Penguin.

Lindsay, C.M. 1969. "Option Demand and Consumer's Surplus." *Quarterly Journal of Economics*, pp. 344–46.

Little, I.M.D., and J.A. Mirrlees. 1974. *Project Appraisal and Planning for the Developing Countries.* New York: Basic Books.

Long, M.F. 1967. "Collective Consumption Services of Individual-Consumption Goods: Comment." *Quarterly Journal of Economics*, pp. 351–52.

Lövemark, O. 1972. "New Approaches to Pedestrian Problems." *Journal of Transport Economics and Policy*, pp. 3–9.

Mansfield, N.W. 1971. "The Estimation of Benefits From Recreation Sites and the Provision of a New Recreation Facility." *Regional Studies*, pp. 56–59.

Mantell, E. 1973. "Suboptimal Land Use Induced by Transportation Planning for New Towns." *Land Economics*, pp. 89–92.

Margolis, J. 1977. "Shadow Prices for Incorrect or Nonexistent Market Values." In R. Haveman and J. Margolis, *Public Expenditure and Policy Analysis.* Chicago: Rand-McNally.

McGuire, M.C., and H.A. Garn. 1969. "The Integration of Equity and Efficiency in Public Project Selection." *Economic Journal*, pp. 882–93.

McKean, R.N. 1968. "The Use of Shadow Prices." In S.B. Chase, ed., *Problems in Public Expenditure Analysis.* Washington, D.C.: Brookings Institution.

Merewitz, L. 1972. "Public Transportation: Wish Fulfillment and Reality in the San Francisco Bay Area." *American Economic Review*, pp. 78–86.

Merewitz, L.; T. Keeler; and P. Fisher. 1975a. *Economic Efficiency in Bus Operations: Preliminary Intermodal Cost Comparisons and Policy Implications.* Berkeley: Institute of Urban and Regional Development, University of California, monograph 19.

———. 1975b. *Automobile Costs and Final Intermodal Cost Comparisons.* Berkeley: Institute of Urban and Regional Development, University of California, monograph 21.

Metro Rail Impact Study. 1975. "Memo to Expert Advisory Panel." Unpublished.

Mills, E. 1966. "Economic Incentives in Air-Pollution Control." In Harold Wolozin, ed., *The Economics of Air Pollution, a Symposium*, pp. 40–50. New York: W.W. Norton and Co.

————. 1972. *Urban Economics*. Glenview, Ill.: Scott, Foresman and Co.

Mishan, E.J. 1967. "Interpretation of the Benefits of Private Transport." *Journal of Transport Economics and Policy*, pp. 184–89.

————. 1970. "What is Wrong with Roskill?" *Journal of Transport Economics and Policy*, pp. 221–34.

————. 1971a. *Cost-Benefit Analysis*. N.Y.: Praeger.

————. 1971b. "Evaluation of Life and Limb: a Theoretical Approach." *The Journal of Political Economy*, pp. 687–705.

Musgrave, R.A. 1969. "Cost-Benefit Analysis and the Theory of Public Finance." *Journal of Economic Literature*, pp. 797–806.

Neuburger, H. 1971. "User Benefit in the Evaluation of Transport and Land Use Plans." *Journal of Transport Economics and Policy*, pp. 52–75.

Nwaneri, V.C. 1970. "Equity in Cost-Benefit Analysis." *Journal of Transport Economics and Policy*, pp. 235–54.

————. 1972. "A Rejoinder." *Journal of Transport Economics and Policy*, p. 325.

Pearce, D.W., and J. Wise. 1972. "Equity in Cost-Benefit Analysis: a Comment." *Journal of Transport Economics and Policy*, pp. 324–25.

Plowden, S.P.C. 1973. "Indirect Taxation of Motorway and Alternative Consumption." *Journal of Transport Economics and Policy*, pp. 250–57.

Polinsky, A., and S. Shavell. 1976. "Amenities and Property Values in a Model of an Urban Area." *Journal of Public Economics*, pp. 119–29.

Prest, A.R., and R. Turvey. 1965. "Cost-Benefit Analysis: a Survey." *Economic Journal*, pp. 683–735.

Ridker, R.G. 1966. "Strategies for Measuring the Cost of Air Pollution." In Harold Wolozin, ed., *The Economics of Air Pollution, a Symposium*, pp. 87–101. New York: W.W. Norton and Co.

(Roskill) Commission on the Third London Airport. 1970. *Papers and Proceedings*. Vol. 7. London: HMSO.

Rothenberg, J. 1965. "Urban Renewal Programs." In A.N. Page and W.R. Seyfried, eds., *Urban Analysis*, pp. 361–87. Glenview, Ill.: Scott, Foresman and Co.

————. 1970. "The Economics of Congestion and Pollution: An Integrated View." *American Economic Review*, pp. 114–21.

Schmalensee, R. 1972. "Option Demand and Consumer's Surplus: Valuing Price Changes Under Uncertainty." *American Economic Review*, pp. 813–24.

————. 1975. "Option Demand and Consumer's Surplus: Reply." *American Economic Review*, pp. 737–39.

Seeley, E.S. Jr. 1972. "Train Occupancy Rate and Facility Optimization in Rapid Transit Systems." *American Economist*, pp. 17–23.

Sherman, R. 1967. "A Private Ownership Bias in Transit Choice." *American Economic Review*, pp. 1211–17.

Shipman, W.D. 1971. "Rail Passenger Subsidies and Benefit-Cost Considerations." *Journal of Transport Economics and Policy*, pp. 3–27.

Smith, E. 1973. "An Economic Comparison of Urban Railways and Express Bus Services." *Journal of Transport Economics and Policy*, pp. 20–31.

Solow, R.M. 1973. "Congestion Cost and the Use of Land for Streets." *Bell Journal*, pp. 602–18.

Squire, L., and H. van der Tak. 1976. *Economic Analysis of Projects*. Baltimore: Johns Hopkins University Press.

Steenbrink, P.A. 1974. *Optimization of Transport Networks*. New York: John Wiley & Sons.

UNIDO (United Nations Industrial Development Organization). 1972. *Guidelines for Project Evaluation*, by P. Dasgupta, A. Sen, and S. Marglin.

Walters, A.A. 1961. "The Theory and Measurement of Private and Social Cost of Highway Congestion." *Econometrica*, pp. 676–99.

Weisbrod, B.A. 1964. "Collective-Consumption Services of Individual-Consumption Goods." *Quarterly Journal of Economics*, pp. 471–77.

——. 1968. "Income Redistribution Effects and Benefit-Cost Analysis." In S.B. Chase, Jr., ed., *Problems in Public Expenditure Analysis*, pp. 177–209. Washington, D.C.: The Brookings Institution.

Westley, G.D. 1976. *The Optimal Location of Urban Radial Rail Lines*. Ph.D. dissertation, University of Pennsylvania.

Wingo, L., Jr., and H.S. Perloff. 1961. "The Washington Transportation Plan: Technics or Politics?" *Papers and Proceedings, Regional Science Association*, pp. 249–62.

Wise, J.; C.B. Chapman; and D.W. Pearce. 1970. "Stage V: Written Evidence to the Roskill Commission on Behalf of the Buckinghamshire County Council. Xerox.

Chapter 3

Demand Analysis

INTRODUCTION

In this chapter an extensive investigation is undertaken into the form that the demand for a suburban rail line is likely to take. Such an investigation has two purposes. The first is to pave the way for the optimal rail line discussion of Chapters 4 and 5. In those chapters it will be necessary to deal with specific mathematical demand relations; investigating the forms such relations might take is one purpose of the analysis undertaken here. The second purpose lies in the crucial and central role that demand plays in the entire scheme of things discussed in this book. Revenue, user benefits, congestion alleviation, and pollution effects depend almost entirely on the demand for line services. Demand also affects nearly every other term mentioned in Chapter 2. The importance of demand for our optimal rail analysis, then, constitutes the second reason for undertaking a demand study.

For reasons of space, no systematic literature review is attempted here. However, comparisons with previous works are made throughout the chapter on a topic-by-topic basis. Readers interested in an integrated and comprehensive survey should consult Allen (1970).

TRIP TYPES INCLUDED AND EXCLUDED: GENERAL SCOPE OF THE ANALYSIS

This chapter presents a theoretical discussion and then an empirical application of the estimation of demand for a certain well-defined class of trips. The empirical example is the Philadelphia-Lindenwold High Speed

Line, a modern technology radial rail line running between the central business district of Philadelphia, Pennsylvania, and Lindenwold, New Jersey.

The HSL opened in January 1969, and as a result, the United States Census, conducted in April 1970, gives a wealth of data on the use of the HSL and competing modes of transportation for the journey to work. In addition, it provides much information on the characteristics of those who used (and who did not use) the line. As is usually the case, data are almost totally lacking (from the census and from any other source) for nonwork trips, and therefore these trips are not dealt with at any great length in this chapter.

The present empirical study is confined to explaining work trips for a given residential and employment pattern. In terms of the trip classification scheme of Chapter 2, the following groups of nonwork journeys are not analyzed empirically: (1) generated trips (i.e., nonwork trips with a new origin and/or destination, undertaken for such purposes as shopping, recreation, downtown cultural visits, seeing friends, etc.); (2) diverted nonwork trips (i.e., nonwork trips now made on the HSL for purposes similar to those in (1), but between the same origin and destination as before); (3) long-run nonwork trips (i.e., those nonwork trips made by people who have changed home and/or job locations and now use the HSL).

As mentioned in Chapter 2, an October 1969 survey of HSL users revealed that 87.6 percent of the trips taken were for purposes of getting to or from work. The fact that nonwork trips are only about 12.4 percent of the total is consolation in the face of the poverty of data about them. In fact, the small share of trips may be considered justification for not engaging in the costly business of predicting explicitly nonwork HSL demand. The data requirements for such predictions are large, and it may prove wiser to take the number of nonwork trips in each of the above three categories as a simple percentage of work trips, as do Foster and Beesley (1963: 76). This shortcut is rendered even less offensive by the fact that most nonwork trips are made at off-peak hours and hence contribute little to reducing congestion, one of the major sources of the benefits of a suburban rail line.

In addition to nonwork trips, this chapter will not deal with prediction of the following types of work trips: (4) long-run commuter trips that begin only after the census was taken in April 1970; (5) reverse haul work trips. The former refers to work trips taken by people who move into the HSL passenger shed after April 1970 (the census takes account of everyone moving into the area before then) and then began to use the line. It can also refer to those who changed job locations after this date and then began to use the HSL. The demand model developed in the later sections of this chapter takes these basic origin and destination data as given. In order to predict residential and employment shifts, a full-scale model of the urban economy is needed. Such models are a recent development and have not yet been used in rail transport planning (though perhaps they should have been). Little more will be said of these models, except that they are the only systematic, general equilibrium approach we have to the complex problem of predicting residential and employment location shifts stemming from the introduction of a suburban rail line in a metropolitan area. Application of the rail demand function, estimated under conditions of given employment and residential location, to these shifts then yields long-run work trip usage of the new rail facility. This, then, is how category (4) should be handled in theory. Whether, in any given situation, a model of the urban area under consideration will exist and will be accurate enough and usable in this context is a practical consideration of great importance. If no such model exists, planners will have to fall back on the usual methodology of employing simple trends, markup relations, and so forth to predict the needed shifts.

Reverse haul work trips refer to work trips that involve commuting in a direction opposite to the main flow of rush hour traffic. In the present case, these are a very small fraction of total trips and so their study has been omitted. However, the theory of modal choice advanced later in this chapter in the context of trips taking place in the usual direction of flow also holds for reverse haul commuters. And the variables used in the empirical application of this theory carry over to the reverse haul case with only a few obvious modifications (e.g., variables representing Philadelphia destinations might be turned around to variables representing New Jersey destinations).

As for estimating generated and diverted nonwork trips—categories (1) and (2) of the omitted trip types—one may employ either an abstract mode model or a traditional hierarchical trip generation—trip distribution—modal split approach.[1] The first method automatically yields closed form demand functions and the second may be modified to do so.[2] This is important, for the optimizing methodology of Chapters 4 and 5 requires closed form demand expressions were we to actually estimate and employ such functions for nonwork trips. Long-run nonwork trips are obtained by employing these equations together with estimates of residential location shifts as well as movements of shopping areas and other attractive centers.

---

[1] See for example Quandt and Baumol (1966, 1969), Mayberry (1970), Quandt and Young (1969), and Gronau and Alcaly (1969) for discussion of the abstract mode approach. And see Brady and Betz (1971), Wilson (1967), and U.S. Department of Transportation (1964, 1965, 1966, 1967), for the traditional hierarchical approach. Westley (1976) discusses some modifications of the abstract mode model to make it more applicable in the intraurban context.

[2] See Westley (1976, ch. 3).

PREDICTION OF RAIL WORK TRIPS FOR
GIVEN RESIDENTIAL AND EMPLOYMENT
PATTERNS: CHOICE OF FUNCTIONAL
FORM AND OTHER CONSIDERATIONS

It must be borne in mind that this book is directed toward the problem of planning the location of an as yet unbuilt rail line. As such, data on usage of the actual line to be built are not available. The reaction of planners to this situation is generally to use demand relations derived from the experience of other cities that have rail lines similar to the one being planned—or at least similar in any characteristics uncontrolled for in the demand function. This will be a satisfactory solution so long as the demand relation used captures the relevant system and user characteristics and, further, so long as the tastes of the two populations after control for these factors are similar. It would be interesting to see a covariance analysis done on several cities to test the degree to which relations derived from interzonal trip-making patterns within a metropolitan area can be used to explain demand in other metropolitan areas.

An improved version of the above method becomes possible to use when a metropolitan area builds a rail system in stages. This allows demand to be observed in one part of the city and derived relations used to forecast demand for the unbuilt links.

Another method that might prove useful in forecasting demand for an unbuilt railroad is the survey method. In the interview, the technological and economic characteristics of the line would be described, and the interviewee's opinion on whether he or she would use the proposed rail line would be solicited. Economic and demographic data thought relevant to explaining the demand would also be collected. While surveys of "buying intentions" are met with mixed feelings by economists (especially when they concern a product not yet available), the value of doing such surveys could grow over time if reinterviews were conducted to determine whether in fact those interviewed used the line. The use of survey data in the presence of a known historical pattern of anticipations and realizations is a much more powerful tool than the survey data alone.

The model of this chapter is, among other things, a contribution toward the first type of approach. By modeling demand for the Lindenwold HSL, we achieve two ends in the current context. First, many hypotheses on the nature of demand are tested; the answers should be of help for rail planners in a wide variety of situations. Second, a mathematical demand relation is derived that can be used with some modifications in other cities planning the construction of a similar high speed modern facility (such as Washington, D.C.,[3] Baltimore, and Atlanta). In addition, the results may

[3] At the time of this writing, Washington is still debating certain route cutbacks. Part of the debate centers around whether there is sufficient demand to justify rail service.

be of interest to rail planners in Philadelphia, who are currently thinking of a two branch extension of the existing HSL. The caveat "with some modifications" is added because data in the same form as used here may not be available in other cities, and so the fitted Philadelphia demand function may have to be reestimated before it can be drafted into use elsewhere. Nevertheless, the use of 1970 census data in this study ought to broaden the intercity transferability of the relations derived because of the common format of data collection.

Now let us turn to the basic question of exactly what our empirical demand model is to explain. Recall that the basic source of data for the Philadelphia study is the 1970 census, taken fifteen months after the opening of the HSL. This gives us cross-section aggregated data on 142 census tracts surrounding the HSL. Census tracts are small geographical zones with an average count of about 4,000 people. Tract boundaries are drawn specifically with the idea of keeping tracts as homogeneous as possible in socioeconomic characteristics, thus providing increased validity to the use of tracts as statistical aggregates.

The census provides data on the choice of mode in the journey to work—giving the number of workers residing in each tract who used bus, auto, or the HSL to commute to work at the time of the census, as well as the number who walked to work, worked at home, or whose method for going to work was listed as "other." (The last is a relatively insignificant category, probably including those who used bicycles, motorcycles, etc.) The explanatory variables of the demand relation are chosen with the idea of predicting HSL usage as it competes with its two main rivals, the auto and bus. The dependent variable in the regression relation is taken as:

$$p = (\text{HSL users})/(\text{HSL users} + \text{auto users} + \text{bus users})$$

—or some monotonic transformation of p (discussed later). This ratio is basically the fraction of potential line users residing in each tract who actually use the HSL.

The universe of potential line users is taken as encompassing only those using the HSL, auto, or bus because, given the relation of residence to workplace, it is doubtful that the line could attract those who work at home or who can walk or bicycle to work, regardless of how good its service is! In view of its small size and the general uncertainty about what the composition of the "other" class is, these workers are also eliminated from the universe of potential line users.

Note that the dependent variable is the ratio of HSL users to potential users rather than merely the number of HSL users (with the number of potential users an added explanatory variable presumably entering in additive fashion on the right-hand side [RHS] of the equation in the latter case). It seems intuitively plausible that if the number of potential users in a tract doubles, while their characteristics remain the same, then HSL ridership should also double. At least this is plausible in the absence of the increased population causing overcrowding or congestion at the HSL stations relative to that caused on other modes—namely, in the absence of "diseconomies of scale." But even if this becomes a real issue (which in our case it is not), these congestion costs can presumably be taken into account in the demand equation. Hence, there seems to be every reason to use ratios instead of levels. Those who use the latter (for example, McDonough [1973] and Foster and Beesley [1963]) make an error of specification. The higher R^2 values generally achieved in such models is, of course, illusory, being due merely to the change in the dependent variable. The ratio form of the model would almost surely do a better job of explaining ridership demand levels as well as ridership rates in both of the above studies.

The next question concerns what the appropriate form of the demand function should be. The simplest relation is, perhaps, the linear one:

$$p = a + \underline{b}\,\underline{x} + u \tag{3.1}$$

where a = a constant term
$\underline{b}$ = a vector of coefficients
$\underline{x}$ = a vector of explanatory variables
u = a stochastic error term.

The choice of explanatory variables will be discussed in the next section, but for now it suffices to say that they are variables such as age; sex; income; auto ownership; time and money costs of using the HSL, bus and car; and destination variables representing the general area of work (e.g., Philadelphia CBD, rest of Philadelphia, etc.).

Before exploring the strengths and weaknesses of the linear as well as of other models, a few important points should be noted concerning this process of demand estimation. The first is that relations estimated at a given time will be used to forecast demand for a new facility for years into the future. As such, it is important to be able to predict basic economic and demographic trends in the area in order to supply values for the explanatory variables and, hence, to allow the HSL demand equation to produce line usage rate forecasts. Thus, it is important to note the trend toward suburbanization of jobs; fewer New Jersey residents working in Philadelphia should affect the values of the destination variables in the equation and hence reduce predictions of line patronage. As another example, since the data we have refer to a time only fifteen months after the opening of the HSL, auto ownership levels may not have been fully adjusted. Possible subsequent reductions should be allowed for. Congestion in the relevant area may increase or decrease and hence affect travel times by bus and car. The age trend in the United States in general is toward a population of higher average age. If this pattern is not significantly altered in the New Jersey area through migration, and if age has a place in the HSL demand equation, this trend should be allowed for. In short, the variables used to explain HSL demand must be projected over time. This includes the denominator of p—that is, the number of workers commuting to work on auto, bus, or rail in each tract. We must do this if we are to get, as is desired, actual HSL use levels (rather than usage rates or fractions). While we may have aggregate population, labor force, employment, and even commutation projections for an entire region or county, breaking these into tract-by-tract projections may require some care. Methods for doing all of the above are outside the scope of the present inquiry.

Using demand relations estimated from cross-section data at a given time for predicting cross-sectional demand at a future time is somewhat dangerous; however, the errors involved may be small compared with the above errors of projecting future changes in explanatory variables. The chief difficulty in using cross-sectional estimates over time is that factors that have not varied in the sample period cross-section may change over time. A notable example is the deterioration of the HSL equipment. In addition, other variables that are difficult to quantify may change: cars may be made in the future so that they become less comfortable relative to the HSL. Or tastes may change either in favor or against use of mass transit in general.

It should be noted (to keep the reader from utter despair) that there is at least limited evidence that cross-sectionally estimated demand relations do change only slowly over time. Brady and Betz (1971) undertook a forecasting experiment in the Phoenix, Arizona, metropolitan area and found that equations are able to forecast travel over a span of at least seven years with a fairly high degree of precision. Nevertheless, travel forecasting is a notoriously risky business, and projections fifty years into the future (a frequently used time horizon for urban rail projects) are bound to have large inaccuracies. The only consolation for our increasing inability to forecast line demand over time is the fact that future costs and benefits, many of which hinge so crucially on demand, will ultimately be reduced at a geometric rate through discounting. It is only to be hoped that our ignorance does not increase faster than the discount factor!

One final point should be made before turning to a discussion of the linear model versus other functional forms. Since the demand equation to be estimated is based on data collected after the opening of the line, it will give us an estimate not only of diverted work trips but also of some long-run work trips. That is, some people will have changed home and/or job locations in anticipation of the line's opening as well as during the fifteen months between the opening of the line and the time of the census. It is important to note that our demand equation will include these long-run as well as diverted users because, as is pointed out in Chapter 2, there is in general a difference in the benefits accruing to each type of user. Were we actually trying to calculate user benefits, it would be necessary to break ridership into diverted and long-run users—perhaps by asking riders who actually used the HSL at census time in 1970 whether they began to use the HSL only as a result of changing home and/or job locations. A positive reply would indicate a long-run rather than diverted user.

The Linear Specification

We turn now to the question of the choice of the functional form with which to estimate the demand relation. Since the variable p is constrained to lie between 0 and 1, it should be clear that the linear form is not an attractive specification. Even if all fitted values of p lie between 0 and 1 in the sample fit, extrapolation to higher costs of a competing mode will eventually drive p above 1, while extrapolation to higher HSL costs will inevitably push p below 0. Similarly, any explanatory variable not itself confined to a limited interval is capable of driving p out of its admissible range.

In addition, the assumption of an additive and normal error term cannot be maintained, since sufficiently large positive or negative drawings of the disturbance would also push p out of the [0,1] interval. Therefore, hypothesis testing based on the usual t, F, and other tests must be viewed as at best approximative in the case of linear regression.

Finally, the linear model has implicit in it some rather counterintuitive behavioral assumptions. The discussion of these will be deferred until later, at which point the contrast with alternative specifications will highlight the problem. Clearly, then, the linear form can at best be an approximation to a more satisfying model. Despite its shortcomings it has been employed in demand estimation work (see, for example, Foster and Beesley [1963] and McDonough [1973]).

The Portmanteau Semilog Specification

A step in the right direction is taken by using the semilog or semilog inverse form for demand, as is done in some studies. A sensible portmanteau combination of these is shown in equation (3.2).

$$log(p) = a - \underline{b}\,\underline{x} - \underline{c}\,1/\underline{z} + u \qquad (3.2)$$

where: $log\ (p)$ = natural logarithm of p ("log" should be read as the natural logarithm throughout the book, unless otherwise noted)

a = a constant term

$\underline{b}, \underline{c}$ = vectors of coefficients, all positive

$\underline{x}, \underline{z}$ = vectors of explanatory variables, all positive

u = a stochastic error term.

Note that p varies inversely with the x type variables and directly with the z type variables. Hence, if a variable is thought to have a negative influence on p, it should be entered into the regression as is, while if it is thought to have a positive effect on p, its inverse should be regressed. These rules are exactly reversed if an explanatory variable has all negative instead of all positive values. The point of regressing variables by the above guidelines is that p is then confined to a limited range, even as the absolute values of the explanatory variables go to infinity. To see this, merely note that the deterministic part of the equation solves to:

$$p = exp(a - \underline{b}\,\underline{x} - \underline{c}\,1/\underline{z}) \tag{3.3}$$

which has a minimum value of 0 and a maximum value of $exp(a)$—where *exp* indicates the exponential function.

While this portmanteau semilog certainly seems an improvement over the linear model, it still has certain problems and drawbacks. First, there is no assurance that the limited range within which p will be bounded is the [0,1] range. It will be this interval if and only if the constant term in the regression is 0. This may indicate the desirability of forcing a to be 0 in semilog demand relations even though this may be mildly restrictive.

Second, if p is to be kept in a limited range, we must use variables that are wholly positive or wholly negative. It is clear from equation (3.3) that if any x or z type variable is allowed to range over the entire real axis, then p will take on all positive values, and the limited range feature of equation (3.2) will be spoiled. This restriction is not too bothersome, since most of the explanatory variables one could think of using are economic and demographic variables, which are generally positive. In fact, the only commonly employed variables that would be taboo in this regard are price and time differences—say between the HSL and competing modes. These differences can be negative (favoring the HSL) or positive (favoring the alternative mode) and hence would spoil the limited range feature of equation (3.2). This constraint can be circumvented by using price and time levels rather than differences.

It should be mentioned in this connection that a third unfortunate feature of the semilog form is that while price and time on the HSL should be entered directly in the equation (as x type variables), price and time for the journey on alternative modes must be entered in inverse form (as z type variables). This implies that we must use price and time ratios, which is not generally desirable (see below) or else (if we do not use ratios, keeping instead separate terms for each mode) that the comparison of price and time effects across modes will be a little strained, as will value of time measurements—as we shall also see in the next section.

Perhaps the major shortcoming of the semilog model, however, lies in its stochastic component. Since p is to be confined to the [0,1] interval, $log(p)$ is confined to the negative half of the real line. Hence equation (3.2) is inconsistent with having the usual additive normal error term, and again, hypothesis testing based on t, F, and similar distributions is at best an approximation, though probably a better one than in the linear model. Note that for generally small values of p (such as occur in our New Jersey sample, in which p is always less than 0.2), the approximation in general will improve, since it requires a fairly large positive draw on the error term to push $log(p)$ above 0, and hence p above 1. This may be very unlikely if the standard error of the disturbance is not too large relative to the size of $log(p)$. Large negative draws on u cannot, of course, force p below 0, and so they lose the sting they carry in the linear model.

It should be pointed out that the problem addressed here in regard to restrictions on the error term, and the resulting approximative nature of hypothesis testing, is rife in economics and largely unaddressed in the econometric literature. It is probably fair to say that most econometric modeling takes place with a dependent variable whose range of values is confined to the positive half of the real line. Yet an additive normal error term is blithely appended to the proposed relation, and hypothesis testing proceeds without the blink of an eyelash. Clearly, in some cases, this may be an acceptable approximation—as when the values that the dependent variable takes on dwarf the standard error of the disturbance term. However, this may not always be the case, and this author believes that a new sampling theory is needed for the case in which the dependent variable is confined and the variance of the disturbance term is large. The assumption of normality cannot be maintained under such circumstances.

The Logit Specification
The next functional form to be considered is the logit—shown in equation (3.4).

$$log\left(\frac{p}{1-p}\right) = a + \underline{b}\,\underline{x} + u \tag{3.4}$$

Note that $p/(1-p)$ represents the odds in favor of riding the HSL and takes on all positive values as p varies from 0 to 1. Taking the log of the odds yields a dependent variable that is a monotonic transformation of p and that ranges over all real numbers. Because of this, the logit is free from all the objections of the linear and portmanteau semilog form.

While we have written the deterministic part of the RHS of equation (3.4) as a linear function of the explanatory variables, we clearly need not do this. Any linear or nonlinear function, $L(x)$, of explanatory variables is acceptable, though we may want to preserve linearity in the parameters to facilitate least squares estimation.

It should not be thought that equation (3.4) is totally free from potential problems. Theil (1971: 635f.) has shown that this form may induce heteroskedasticity in the error term. This is discussed below; however, it presents no great obstacle to econometric estimation. Generalized least squares procedures are merely used in place of ordinary least squares (OLS).

The equation of the logit can be solved for p. Suppressing the stochastic component we get:

$$p = e^{L(x)}/[1 + e^{L(x)}] \tag{3.5}$$

or equivalently,

$$p = 1/[1 + e^{-L(x)}] \tag{3.6}$$

Graphing p versus the index of explanatory variables, $L = L(x)$, we get an S-shaped curve, as shown in Figure 3–1. Note that the point of inflection occurs at $p = 0.5$. At this point, a given change in any of the explanatory variables has the greatest impact on rail use. The plausibility of this assumption in the context of our aggregate cross-section model is examined below.[4]

While the logit (and probit) functions have been widely used in work trip demand studies, their application has been basically confined to the case where the data is on an individual rather than zonally aggregated basis. The well-known studies of Warner (1962), Lisco (1967), and Lave (1970) all use data on individual decisions on the journey to work and use a logit or probit (or discriminant) analysis to explain modal choice. In such applications, use of the standard probit or logit form is behaviorally

---

[4] A curve very similar in shape, though more complex in form, is the probit. The similarity in shape between the logit and probit, together with the difficulty of estimating (nonlinear maximum likelihood techniques must be used) and subsequently manipulating the probit form, lead to favoring the logit over the probit in further work in this chapter.

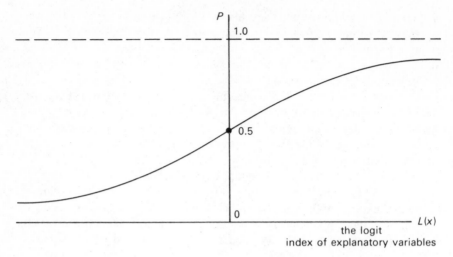

Figure 3-1.   The S-Shaped Curve of the Logit.

sensible. Both imply that if a person is just on the edge of indecision (i.e., if there is a fifty-fifty chance that the rail line will be chosen), a given change in $L(x)$ or $M(x)$ will have a larger impact than if the person has a fairly sure idea of which mode he or she prefers.

However, what works at the individual level may not be as appropriate at the zonal level, even though it is sometimes used there. It seems much more of an open question whether a given change in an independent variable would have a greater effect when 50 percent of the potential HSL users in a tract are actually riding the HSL than at any other usage rate. In fact, there is good evidence in the present context for thinking that the point of maximum influence (i.e., the inflection point) is at a much lower value than $p = 0.5$.

The Compressed Logit Specification

The 1970 census data reveal that even in the highest use tract, only 18.9 percent of potential users rode the HSL (i.e., the maximum value of p that is observed is 0.189). The basic reason for usage rates this low is that the workplace of most of the residents of the New Jersey tracts is not easily accessible from the HSL. Trip end costs, therefore, put a large majority of potential HSL users "out of the market" for HSL services.

What all of this points to is that, given residential and employment patterns as well as the existing downtown distribution system, the HSL can only aim, in general, at attracting a minority fraction of potential riders in each tract. As a result, the level of p at which the greatest aggregate indecision between the HSL and competing modes is felt is most probably at values much less than 0.5. Illustrating again with typical numbers from the New Jersey case, it seems likely that in tracts where the HSL has perhaps only 0.5 percent of the potential users, a 25¢ (or approximately 50 percent) drop in fares is not likely to increase this percentage greatly. The line is so uncompetitive with other modes that few people will be stimulated to "jump on board" under such a fare change. On the other hand, a 25¢ or even smaller drop in fares may yield a much larger rise in p in tracts where p is already 5 percent. For in tracts where p is 5 percent, the HSL is likely to be a fairly competitive mode, having already garnered, in all probability, a good percentage of all the riders who are potentially "in the market" for its services.

In view of these arguments, one might want a functional form that is shaped like the logit but that has its inflection point at a p value other than 0.5. One possibility is explored in this book, the deterministic part of the equation being:

$$p = c/[1 + e^{-L(x)}] \qquad (3.7)$$

where c is a constant whose value is less than 1. This form shall be called the compressed logit (or c logit) and c dubbed the degree of compression.

The c logit is S-shaped like the logit, but the point of maximum impact has now been moved down to $p = c/2$, where c is a scalar that should probably lie between 0 and 1 (since p is confined to the $(0,c)$ interval). In more complex formulations, which will not be pursued here, c can be made a function of observable variables together with unknown parameters.

Like the logit, the c logit can also be estimated by least squares after some transformations. The required manipulation is:

$$1 - p = [1 - c + e^{-L(x)}]/[1 + e^{-L(x)}] \qquad (3.8)$$

Hence,

$$\frac{1-p}{p} = \frac{1-c}{c} + \frac{1}{c} e^{-L(x)} \qquad (3.9)$$

And finally, adding a stochastic error:

$$\log \left(\frac{1-p}{p} - \frac{1-c}{c} \right) = -\log c - L(x) + u \qquad (3.10)$$

Comparison of Behavioral Assumptions

It is instructional to compare the cross-tract behavioral assumptions of the linear, semilog, and logit type (logit and c logit) models. To fix ideas, suppose we consider dropping HSL fares by 30¢. In one (high use) tract, suppose ridership rises from 10 percent to 15 percent—a 50 percent increase in HSL use. Consider now what would happen if we dropped fares by 30¢ in a low use tract, say with 1 percent ridership. The linear model says that p should rise to 6 percent—the same absolute increase in p for the same change in fares. This would seem a dubious result, since if ridership is only 1 percent, most nonriders are probably pretty firmly entrenched as *non*users of the HSL. The linear model seems to be implicitly counterintuitive.

The semilog model is more reasonable. It purports that a given change in fares should have the same proportional effect on all tracts. If p rises from 10 percent to 15 percent in one tract, it ought to rise from 1 to about 1.5 percent in another. This is much more in line with the idea that few commuters in the low use tract will be on the edge of indecision between the HSL and an alternative mode, and hence few will be persuaded to come over to the HSL when fares drop by 30¢.

The logit and c logit models yield results much closer to the semilog than to the linear model. For example, taking the logit, a change from 10 to 15 percent ridership represents a rise in odds in favor of riding the HSL from 1/9 to 3/17. This is a 37 percent rise in the odds in favor of riding the HSL. This implies an increase in ridership in the low use tract from 1 percent to about 1.36 percent. The behavioral difference between the logit type models and the semilog is that in the latter, the effect of a given change in an explanatory variable has the same percentage effect on p regardless of the level of p, whereas in the logit type models, the percentage effect on p is greatest in a certain critical region (i.e., around the inflection point) and diminishes as one moves away from this area.

These are the four basic forms that will be considered in the empirical demand analysis that follows. One could certainly think of other limited range functions that might serve as candidates. For example:

$$log(p) = a - b \, log(1 + e^x) - c \, log(1 + e^{\frac{1}{z}}) + u \qquad (3.11)$$

is a limited range demand form with properties similar to the portmanteau semilog. Alternatively, the principal part of the inverse tangent function could be pressed into service—being an S-shaped, fixed range function. These will not be explored here; rather, we pass on to a consideration of the independent variables that should enter on the RHS of the demand relation. This is the topic of the next section.

PREDICTION OF RAIL WORK TRIPS FOR GIVEN RESIDENTIAL AND EMPLOYMENT PATTERNS: CHOICE OF EXPLANATORY VARIABLES

In this section we examine the types of explanatory variables that might be used in our demand model. The next section explores econometric issues relevant to the current task, while the final section presents the empirical evidence and serves to give precise, technical definitions to variables. Many of the alternative definitions of variables will not be mentioned in this section so that a broader and more concept-oriented picture may be painted.

Age, Sex, and Homeownership— Factors Affecting the Utility Functions of Commuters

These variables are in scattered use in various demand studies. The theoretical justification for including them is that they affect the utility function of the potential HSL user. Lave (1970), for example, finds that older workers tend to prefer driving over rapid transit, perhaps to avoid as much walking as possible. Many investigators have found that a higher female fraction of potential users has a significant positive effect on public transit usage (see, for example, Lisco [1967] and Kain [1964]). Kain (1964) also finds that single family dwellers are more likely to be auto users, ceteris paribus, than those living in multiple family or apartment units. Actually, this may be because the single family dweller is a different kind of person (the utility argument) or because owning a home (and garage) allows easier use of a car (a cost argument). These three concepts will be tested in our HSL equation.

Auto Availability—The Person/Auto Ratio

Variables like this are common in demand studies, having, of course, a positive impact on line usage. Kain (1964) finds such a variable significant, as does McDonough (1973), at least in most of the cases she examines.

There are two reasons for entering such a variable. First, a high auto availability ratio may indicate a strong preference on the part of commuters for using the auto. This is a variation in the utility function line of argument. Second, a high tract auto availability ratio may indicate that more families in the tract would have bought one or more of their cars anyway, for nonwork purposes. In such a case, the true cost of driving to work in this tract will be closer to the marginal cost (MC) of auto use (i.e., excluding insurance, depreciation due to age, etc.) than the average cost (AC). Since in the calculations per mile auto costs are, of necessity, taken to be the same in all tracts (since the required data on reason for car purchase is not available), auto ownership then may act as proxy for correcting the relative amounts of this MC-AC discrepancy across tracts.

It should be noted that while motorists are notorious for underperceiving the true cost of their auto trip, it still is likely that perceived MC will nevertheless be lower than perceived AC, due to the fact that actual MC is substantially less than actual AC. Hence the force of auto availability is left intact. Another point is that while a higher auto availability may "reduce" the cost of using the auto for getting to work, it will also reduce the cost of reaching HSL stations by auto (the auto being the access mode actually used by the vast majority of HSL users). However, since auto commuters use their car over the entire length of the journey to work, while HSL users employ it only for shorter distances, high auto availability still tends to give a cost advantage to the car commuters and hence to reduce HSL usage. That is, the usual direction of impact on HSL usage remains, even in the face of the above argument.

Income—As a Separate
Explanatory Variable

As we shall see below, income will most likely interact with time spent riding each mode, in order to allow for variations in the value of time. It may also interact with price in a way that postulates that as income rises, the money cost of a mode becomes a less important determinant of modal choice. But income may also enter the equation as a separate term. This last use for income is discussed here.

There are two reasons why income might enter the demand equation as a separate term, and these parallel the reasons why auto ownership might be an explanatory variable. First, however, we note one traditional role that income will not play here. Since the quantity of journey to work trips is largely an institutionally set amount for the vast majority of HSL users, income cannot play its usual role of affecting the quantity purchased of a good—namely, the number of work trips made. Illustrative of this fixedness is the traditional practice (followed here) of predicting the number of people who will use the HSL for work trips and then relying on the above inelasticity to derive by simple multiplication the number of work trips made on the HSL.

What then are the reasons for entering income as a separate variable? The first is, again, that differences in income levels may indicate differences in utility functions. One could think of many underlying sociological factors; here are a few. Richer people may prefer the HSL more than poorer people because it may be more important to the former group to be able to sit quietly and read a newspaper; or to have time to contemplate and collect thoughts before work; or because in their circle of friends, riding the HSL is the "educated thing to do" in view of social problems such as pollution and congestion known to be caused by automobiles (see Allen [1970: 128], where some evidence for this third effect is cited). Conversely, poorer people may prefer to drive in order to show off their cars or because driving is a status symbol for this group. Both lists could be extended, and both point to income having a positive effect (ceteris paribus) on HSL ridership. Sociological factors could also be advanced that would support income having a negative effect on HSL ridership; however, these are generally more strained and not as often mentioned in the literature.

The second reason for including income is that if a poor person does own a car, it is more likely that she or he bought that car to use in the work journey. While if a wealthier person owns a car she or he may choose to own it independent of which mode is used to get to work. This means that the poorer person must impute the average cost of car ownership per mile in calculating the cost of the auto journey, while the richer person need only impute the marginal costs (yearly depreciation, insurance, etc. will be paid independent of how she or he chooses to travel to work). Like higher auto availability, then, higher income will exert a negative influence (ceteris paribus) on HSL ridership according to the above logic. Note that this second reason calls for income to enter with the opposite sign than the very first group of "utility" type stories called for. With these conflicting forces, it will be most interesting to see if a separate income term is significant and, if so, in which direction its influence goes.

Previous empirical evidence suggests that a separate income term may have a positive effect on rail use. In their study of Chicago, CATS (1973) finds this, though the income term is statistically quite insignificant. However, in the study neither the interaction between time and income nor between price and income are allowed for, which makes even an insignificant positive sign on the separate income term surprising. To see why this is so, note that as income rises, a person's value of time (VOT) is generally expected to rise, and so the person is more likely to choose the faster mode, which is, in the Chicago case, the car. Therefore rising income would be expected to reduce the importance of the cost advantage that rail has over the auto; and thus, rising income should produce falling rail ridership. The fact that CATS does not control for these effects (as we do here) and still gets income positively affecting rail ridership speaks very strongly for the utility type of arguments.

Housing Costs and Supernumerary Income

Subtracting rent payments or homeownership costs from household income yields what will be called in this chapter supernumerary income. Why might we want to use this measure instead of total income?

The reason is that since the census data were taken at a time only fifteen months after the opening of the HSL, some households were undoubtedly in consumer's disequilibrium with respect to housing expenditures. That is, since substitution of the HSL for the car for the journey to work, in general, reduces commuting costs (while substitution of the HSL for the bus increases such costs), the opening of the HSL alters the amount that many rail commuters spend on their work trips. However, since the decision to relocate to new quarters is one that is often slowly made and implemented, many consumers may be spending more or less for housing than their desired equilibrium amount. As a result, we may prefer to use supernumerary income (SY) in place of income alone (Y) for interacting with modal prices. That is, a commuter may give more or less weight to the cost advantage that the HSL has over the auto according to supernumerary income, not actual income.

While SY may do better than Y in interactions with price, there seems to be little reason to prefer SY over Y as a separate income term. Certainly Y seems the more natural concept relating to utility considerations; however, SY may be the more pertinent indicator of whether a car is bought independent of the journey to work.

As for income indicating the value of time (VOT), Y again is the usual concept. However, the classical argument for using Y, that it indicates the value of what could have been earned in an extra hour of work, is somewhat oversimplified in the present context for at least two reasons, as will be discussed below. The value of time spent riding to work can at best, under modern theory, be thought to be correlated with income, rather than equal to it. As recent, post-Becker work on the allocation of time clearly points out (see, for example, DeSerpa (1971: eq. 3.1), the value of time in an activity will also depend on the dollar amount spent on all goods. However, the relationship is highly nonlinear, and there is no reason to think, therefore, that SY will be more highly correlated with VOT than Y, even though it includes the amount spent on housing. In summary, the advisability of using SY instead of Y remains an open question, subject to empirical testing. And it may be more appropriate at some points in the equation than in others.

Destination Variables

While the census does not provide detailed destination data on a tract-by-tract basis, it does provide broad indicators of workplace. These statistics give the percentage of all workers working in the Philadelphia CBD, the rest of Philadelphia, and Camden County. All of the above should have a positive influence on HSL usage.

Walk Access to the HSL

The vast majority of users in 1970 reached the HSL by car. Accordingly, access costs are computed assuming the auto mode of access. (Use is made of a survey, taken on the same day as the census by Drs. D.

Boyce and W. B. Allen, which reveals the exact type of car access—free parker, pay parker, or kiss-n-rider—as well as station choice. These survey results are used in the computation of HSL time and money cost).

However, a limited number of tracts have neighborhoods within walking distance of HSL stations. "Within walking distance" is taken as 3,000 feet, a measure that, according to Lövemark (1972), is about the maximum walking distance a commuter is willing to endure. A dummy variable is entered, then, taking on a value of 1 if the tract has at least 10 percent of its residential blocks within 3,000 feet of a HSL station and 0 otherwise.

Price and Time Variables

The starting points for discussion are the simplistic difference specifications of price and time used by Lisco (1967) and CATS (1973). The explanatory variables used there are $(P_r - P_0)$ and $(T_r - T_0)$—where P_r and P_0 are the money prices of using the rail and another mode, while T_r and T_0 are the journey times by rail and the other mode, respectively. In our case, since we are considering two modal competitors to the HSL instead of just one, we would use four explanatory variables. While there is room for choice about which variables are repeated, they might be: $(P_r - P_a)$, $(P_r - P_b)$, $(T_r - T_a)$, $(T_r - T_b)$—where the subscripts a and b indicate auto and bus, while r indicates the HSL (rail). Several comments follow on the advisability of using this set of explanatory variables.

The first is that it is almost certainly an unforgivable misspecification to use straight time differences. It is widely accepted that a high income commuter values time more highly than a low income commuter. In fact, the classical argument is that the value of time (VOT) spent in an activity (such as commuting) is equal to the wage rate. While this is an oversimplification for at least two reasons, it will nevertheless emerge that a far superior specification to simple time differences is time differences multiplied by income (or some simple function of income). To see this, we must first note the objections.

The first objection to the classical model is undertaken by Moses and Williamson (1963). Their argument is that since the length of the work week is institutionally set for most workers, most workers are not free at the margin to trade time for wage earnings. Hence, the classical equality between the VOT and the wage rate disintegrates. Further, Moses and Williamson argue, if a person desires to work more than the institutionally set work week it must be that his or her VOT is less than the wage rate, while the reverse is true of those persons wanting to work less than they currently do. While Moses and Williamson certainly make a step in the right direction, their model, based only on amending the classics to account for the institutionalized work week, is also open to objection. The nature of the second objection can be traced at least as far back as

Adam Smith's *The Wealth of Nations* (Book 1, Chapter 10). There Smith states that one cause of wage differentials is the "varying disagreeableness" of different tasks. Applying this principle to our case, we see that saving a dollar by spending an extra fifteen minutes commuting may be much preferred to obtaining that dollar by working an extra 15 minutes (were the latter institutionally feasible). Therefore, the VOT in the journey to work need not equal the wage rate, because commuting and working may vary in their "disagreeableness." Commuting is generally thought to be less disagreeable, a hypothesis that would account for the frequently made empirical finding that the VOT is only a small fraction of the wage rate (usually between 1/5 and 1/2).

While there is no strict relation between the value of commutation time and income, it is intuitive that there still should be a fairly strong correlation. It is confirmed in studies on the determinants of the value of time (see Lee and Dalvi [1969, 1971]) that this is indeed the case. That is, if one can save ten minutes in the journey to work, this will be weighted much more heavily by a high income person than by a low income person. Multiplication of the simple time differentials by income or some function of income is therefore indicated. The exact form of the time-income interaction is a topic for further discussion below. However, to fix ideas for the reader, one may visualize the improved version of the specification as being represented by:

$$(P_r - P_a), (P_r - P_b), kY(T_r - T_a), kY(T_r - T_b) \qquad (3.12)$$

where Y indicates income, and k a constant. This embodies what is perhaps the simplest assumption, that the VOT is proportional to income.

The next objection, even to this improved specification, is that the use of price and time differentials may be unduly restrictive. These differentials are widely used in demand studies—notably by Lave (1970) as well as by Lisco (1967) and CATS (1973). To see the nature of the objection, suppose we posit a demand model (be it linear, semilog, logit, c logit, or whatever) in which the four independent variables listed above enter on the right-hand side in additive fashion. This corresponds to what is done in almost all demand studies. Letting z represent the price and time terms in the equation we have:

$$z = a_1(P_r - P_a) + a_2(P_r - P_b) + b_1 Y(T_r - T_a) + b_2 Y(T_r - T_b) \qquad (3.13)$$

Suppose the Ps are measured in cents, the Ts in minutes, and Y in cents per minute. A decrease in auto time (T_a) by one minute will have an effect on z (and hence on the dependent variable) of $b_1 Y$. This can be exactly offset by raising the cost of auto travel (P_a) by $(b_1/a_1)Y$ cents. That is, the

VOT saving (or loss) in an auto journey is $(b_1/a_1)Y$ cents per minute. It can be argued along the same lines that the VOT in a bus journey is $(b_2/a_2)Y$ cents per minute. It is sensible that the VOT spent in bus and car should be allowed to differ, as they do here, since the modes may differ in comfort and other unmeasured amenities.

The problem comes when we look at the value of time spent on rail. Raising T_r by one minute raises z by $(b_1+b_2)Y$, implying a VOT on rail of

$$\left(\frac{b_1+b_2}{a_1+a_2}\right)Y. \text{ Since this equals } \left[\frac{b_1}{a_1}(Y)\right]\left(\frac{a_1}{a_1+a_2}\right) + \left[\frac{b_2}{a_2}(Y)\right]\left(\frac{a_2}{a_1+a_2}\right),$$

and since the terms in brackets are the VOTs on car and bus, we see that the VOT on rail is merely a weighted average of the former two VOTs.

A further, less subtle, restriction that the use of equation (3.13) implies is that a 1¢ increase in fares on the HSL has the same effect as a 1¢ reduction in the cost of using both auto and bus. And similarly a one minute drop in T_r has the same effect on ridership as a one minute rise in each of T_a and T_b together. Like the VOT restriction, these assertions are strong ones and need to be tested. One would alter the details but not the fundamental nature of these restrictions by using some other set of differences.

If, of course, the assertions are correct, one would want to retain the difference form in order to improve the efficiency of estimation. It is not likely, in the view of this author, that all these restrictions are, in most situations, correct. There seems to be no reason to believe that the value of time spent riding one mode should be a neat weighted average of the VOT of riding the two competing modes. The amenities provided by each may not make for conformance to such a scheme.

In order to remove all of the above restrictions, it is only necessary to use price and time levels in place of differences. That is, we would have:

$$z = a_1P_r+a_2P_a+a_3P_b+b_1(Y\cdot T_r)+b_2(Y\cdot T_a)+b_3(Y\cdot T_b) \tag{3.14}$$

It is easily verified that all restrictions are removed and that the VOTs on HSL, auto, and bus are b_1/a_1, b_2/a_2, and b_3/a_3, respectively.

Two hybrids of equations (3.13) and (3.14) may prove useful, with a view toward reducing problems of multicollinearity. They are:

$$z = a_1P_r+a_2P_a+a_3P_b+b_1Y(T_r-T_a)+b_2Y(T_r-T_b) \tag{3.15}$$

and,

$$z = a_1(P_r-P_a)+a_2(P_r-P_b)+b_1(Y\cdot T_r)+b_2(Y\cdot T_a)+b_3(Y\cdot T_b) \tag{3.16}$$

It can be readily verified in both equations (3.15) and (3.16) that the VOTs on HSL, auto, and bus are free to vary independently of each other. The only restriction equation (3.15) implies that equation (3.14) does not is that an equal absolute rise in travel time on all three modes has no effect on ridership. Equation (3.16) implies a similar restriction with respect to an equal increase in money cost on all three modes. While equations (3.15) or (3.16) may be useful for statistical reasons, we shall take equation (3.14) as the best "newly improved version" of the price and time variables, for purposes of further discussion.

Before proceeding, however, the reader's attention should be called to a rather remarkable phenomenon. By using equation (3.14) we have, to a large extent, succeeded in quantifying the seemingly unquantifiable. Few, if any measures exist of the relative comfort, aesthetics, perceived safety, and so forth of the various modes. Yet by allowing for intermodal differences in the value of time, we have captured just these intangibles and have captured them in a way that reduces them all to a single value of time number!

The procedure is exact to the extent that the effect of each of these intangibles rises proportionately to (i.e., is exactly collinear with) time spent. It is approximative, but still a very useful aggregative indicator, if this condition is violated. I would comment that the required condition does not seem at all unreasonable: comfort or discomfort effects (e.g., seat versus no seat, presence or absence of air conditioning, etc.) ought to increase about as time spent on the mode does. So should the aesthetic effects of the trip (loud noises, noxious odors, etc.). Variability of travel time, another factor that is rarely calculated (as is true in this study), may also increase proportionately with trip time. Safety is probably more related to distance than time, but the two are, in general, highly correlated anyway.

While it would, in the absence of perfect collinearity with time, be even better to have exact data on all these intangibles, this is impossible. Use of an equation like (3.14) is a practical tool of great importance. It is an unfortunate fact that so many researchers have overlooked this important point and have opted for use of price and time differences rather than levels. (It is especially unfortunate in cases dealing with the choice between only two modes—because of the highly restrictive implication of equal VOTs!) A notable exception to this widespread deficiency is Quarmby (1967).

The next point to be made about the specification of the price and time terms involves what I shall call the value of time fraction (VOTF). The VOTF for a mode is simply a number that when multiplied by the wage rate gives the VOT for riding the mode. In equation (3.14), for example, the VOTFs for the HSL, auto, and bus are b_1/a_1, b_2/a_2, and b_3/a_3, respectively. That is, so far our model has postulated VOTFs that are constant with respect to income. There are a couple of reasons to think that such may not be the case.

It might be casually observed that high income executives or professional types often are in the position of having a job in which they are expected to put in well over forty hours per week. With similar casualness, we note that lower income factory and assembly line workers, and secondary laborers in general, usually have a work week much more in the thirty-six to forty hours per week range. It may well be that, given this variation in the length of the institutionalized work week, and given the way this length varies with income, the poor are work preferrers and the rich are leisure preferrers. That is, if institutions could be changed, the poor would opt for more work and the rich for more leisure. If this is the case, and if, for simplicity of illustration, riding the HSL were just as distasteful as work for all income classes, we would find the HSL VOTF to be greater than 1 for the rich and smaller than 1 for the poor. Putting the result more generally: if the rich would like a bigger cut in their work week relative to the poor, we expect to find VOTFs rising with income. While "bigger relative cut" may be difficult to quantify, the principle is clear enough.

A second possible reason for the VOTF to vary with income lies in the chance that wage differentials do not fully reflect the varying disagreeableness of the work performed by different income classes. It may be that the higher paid executives and professionals enjoy their work greatly, but due to market imperfections (e.g., imperfect knowledge of the situation, the desire to propagate the tenet that the work they do is "hard"—see Galbraith [1969], institutionalized practices, etc.) are not "penalized" fully for this in the wage they earn. Hence, they truly benefit from the pleasantness of their jobs. On the other hand, the work of the lower income classes is generally more disagreeable. But it may be that through the operation of market forces (and labor unions), there is complete compensation for this. If the above is the case, then again, we will find the VOTF rising as money income does. That is, the rich will require that a higher fraction of their money wage be paid them for spending an extra minute in commutation, since relative to the poor, commuting is less pleasant than work. One could certainly think of scenarios that would justify a negative, rather than positive, relation between VOTF and income. And even more complicated relations, with the direction of correlation changing one or even several times, are possible.

There is no hard evidence on whether workers, or a subgroup of workers (classified by occupational type or income) have wage differentials that compensate for differing degrees of arduousness in work. Because of this, all scenarios seem possible, including ones where VOTF varies not only with income, but also with job type at the given income level.

Whether or not there is a relation between the VOTF and income becomes, then, a matter for empirical investigation. The evidence to date is very limited. The only study, Quarmby (1967), finds that VOTF is relatively constant over a wide range of income. The case is far from closed, however.

There are many possibilities for modeling VOTF as a function of income. A few of the most basic are perhaps (without specifying whether c, d, and e are positive or negative):

$$VOTF = c + dY$$
$$VOTF = c + dY^{1/2}$$
$$VOTF = c + d/Y$$
$$VOTF = c + dY + eY^2$$

The first posits a strictly linear relation, the second tests whether VOTF might rise more slowly with income than in the first, and the third tests for an inverted relation. The fourth allows the relation to be positive over one part of the income range and negative over the rest.

Modifying equation (3.14) to allow for the first of these possibilities, we get:

$$z = a_1 P_r + a_2 P_a + a_3 P_b + (c_1 + d_1 Y)Y \cdot T_r + (c_2 + d_2 Y)Y \cdot T_a + \\ (c_3 + d_3 Y)Y \cdot T_b. \quad (3.17)$$

Other VOTF expressions can be similarly substituted.

Another alteration of equation (3.14) we may wish to consider is allowing the importance of price or price differentials on modal choice to diminish with income. This certainly seems intuitively reasonable. A 30¢ difference in fare levels is less of a consideration to a high income commuter than to a low income commuter. To help fix ideas, I suggest a few possibilities. Letting P_i stand for the price level of each mode (or price differences) we might try[5]: P_i/Y, $P_i/Y^{1/2}$, $P_i(a-bY)$.

Another variant on equation (3.14) that should be tested is whether the time variables ought to be raised to a power other than 1. Letting T_i represent each of the time variables in equation (3.14), we might consider trying $T_i^{1/2}$, $T_i^{3/2}$, T_i^2. The first choice represents the hypothesis that a journey becomes less arduous as it goes on. Or to put it another way, the

---

[5] Note that using these three price expressions instead of P_i, multiplies the value of time (VOT) and value of time fraction (VOTF) by Y, $Y^{1/2}$, and $(a-bY)^{-1}$, respectively.

last ten minutes of a thirty minute journey is less of a burden than the preceding ten minutes or the first ten minutes. The last two choices ($T_i^{3/2}$ and T_i^2) represent the opposite side of the argument. There has been some debate about which of these points of view is the correct one, though with little being resolved. No modal choice models, to my knowledge, have ever incorporated time raised to any power other than 1. The time has come to test this steadfastness (or oversight).

The next question to be considered does not concern an alteration in the form of equation (3.14). Rather, it deals with the question of how (and whether) to aggregate different kinds of time in order to produce a total time of commutation by each mode. This will be examined empirically below. In previous studies of the question (and there have been many— e.g., Goldberg [1963], Quarmby [1967], Pratt [1970]) it is generally found that walking, waiting, and transferring time are implicitly valued by the commuter at two to three times in-vehicle time. For convenience, walking, waiting, and transfer time will be termed "hard time," while in-vehicle time will be termed "easy time."

One final type of journey time, infrequently mentioned in the literature and never to my knowledge used in a demand study, is what will be called here schedule delay time. It is really only relevant to bus commutation, where headways on some routes are large. The idea is that if a worker must get into Philadelphia by 8:30 for work and if there are buses arriving there only at 8:15 and 8:45 (thirty minute headway), then the passenger will be forced to arrive fifteen minutes earlier than necessary. In all probability, the worker will not be compensated for the early arrival, and so it represents a loss. The loss may be tempered if the worker is satisfied to be at work and to read or socialize or can find some other satisfying prework activity. As a result, we might suspect, a priori, that schedule delay time should be weighted less than in-vehicle (easy) time.

There is no schedule delay time for a lone auto driver. There may be some for carpoolers, but as the average auto occupancy ratio in the tracts under study is only 1.15, it is not felt that schedule delay time is significant enough for auto users to warrant an attempt at calculation. Similarly, schedule delay time is considered negligible for HSL users, since trains ran every five or seven and one-half minutes during the peak periods of 1970. Schedule delay data are calculated, then, only for the New Jersey system buses.

The method for calculating delay time proposed here is somewhat arbitrary, but it is the first attempt at quantification and hopefully contains elements of realism. The first step is to derive from the bus schedules an average headway time, denoted as h. In the above example this would be thirty minutes. Next we make two assumptions. The first is that at least some of the workers have some flexibility on when they can arrive at work. That is, while part of the group must be absolutely on time to punch a clock, another part need not be so punctual. An average grace period of five minutes is assumed—namely, that, on average, workers may arrive up to five minutes after the "start" of work with no penalty. This is only an educated guess, though one based on many experiences and much discussion. Second, since Boyce and Allen (1972) find that there are multiple work peaks in Philadelphia, it was decided to make the simplifying assumption that bus runs are essentially random with respect to work starting times—over the small range of times we will consider.

Putting these elements together, it is straightforward to show that expected or average schedule delay time is given by:

$$SDT = \left(1 - \frac{5}{h}\right)(1/2)(h-5) = \frac{(h-5)^2}{2h} = \frac{h}{2} - 5 + \frac{25}{2h} \tag{3.18}$$

This is illustrated in Figure 3–2, assuming a headway of thirty minutes and a starting time of 8:30. Under the assumed five minutes grace, the worker can arrive anywhere between 8:30 and 8:35 with no penalty. The earliest she or he will arrive is 8:05, suffering twenty-five minutes of delay time. Assuming the buses run randomly with respect to starting time, expected schedule delay time is: (5/6) (12.5) + (1/6) 0 = 10 5/12 minutes.

A final alteration of equation (3.14) that we might consider is the use of price and time ratios instead of levels or differences. While some investigators have used ratios in the past, notably Warner (1962), the use of levels, rather than ratios, seems to this author to be the correct choice. The reason is well illustrated by Allen (1970: 124). His argument is that the

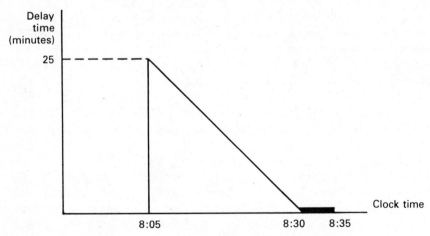

Figure 3–2. Average Schedule Delay Time.

ratio approach would imply that a car fare of $1 and a HSL fare of $.50 would have the same effect as a car fare of $50 and a HSL fare of $25—since both correspond to a relative price of two. Similarly, it would imply that time levels of ten minutes versus five minutes and two hours versus one hour should be treated as equivalent. Clearly, they are not equivalent. Since the quantity of work trips is an institutionally fixed number for the vast majority of commuters, the only choice that remains is how to make the trips. Here differences in (or more precisely, levels of) price, time, and amenities are clearly the deciding factors. This is unlike the case usually dealt with in consumer demand theory, in which the number of goods has yet to be decided, with relative prices (and income) playing a decisive role.

Having completed our survey on the choice of explanatory variables, we turn now to a brief consideration of econometric issues relevant to estimating the required demand function.

PREDICTION OF RAIL WORK TRIPS FOR GIVEN RESIDENTIAL AND EMPLOYMENT PATTERNS: ECONOMETRIC ISSUES

In this section, three areas are dealt with: heteroskedasticity, use of the Durbin Watson (d) statistic to test for omitted explanatory variables and errors in variables, and testing the significance of one predictor over another.

Heteroskedasticity

It is common for cross-section studies to suffer from heteroskedasticity. In order to test for its presence and subsequently to reestimate the regression using a feasible Aitken procedure in place of OLS, we must postulate a systematic formula for the variance of the error term. Two possible formulas are suggested here.

The first assumes that heteroskedasticity is introduced by using observations in which there are a different number of potential users in each census tract. Specifically, it may be easier to explain the fraction of rail users in tracts with a large number of potential users than in tracts where this number is small. This is because increasing aggregation may wash out, to a greater degree, the part of the disturbance term that is due to randomness in human behavior (i.e., the tendency of individuals to not act according to any population model). Some support for this is found in the fact that demand equations fitted on individualistic data generally have a lower R^2 (explained variance percentage) than models using zonally aggregated data. One seems to be able to explain group behavior better than individual behavior. Whether this will imply that it is easier to explain large group behavior than small group behavior is the issue that will be tested here (potential users per tract vary in our sample from about 300 to 5,000).

Another strand of possible support for this form of heteroskedasticity, at least in the linear model, comes from the fact that when there is a micro (individual level) model of behavior, which is then aggregated to group means, heteroskedasticity is induced and is of the type suggested— assuming the micromodel is of the classical (homoskedastic) type. The problem is that while one can think of approximations or proxies, it seems impossible to establish exactly the corresponding individualistic concepts for some of the aggregate explanatory variables, such as persons per auto. As a result, the above theorem on the errors of grouped mean equations may have limited relevance, even for the linear model.

A second possible form that heteroskedasticity may take is derived by Theil (1971: 635ff.) for the logit model. The form is:

$$Var(U_i) = k^2/n_i p_i(1-p_i),$$

where U_i = error in the ith tract
n_i = number of potential users in the ith tract
p_i = fraction of potential users riding the HSL in the ith tract
k = a constant.

This contrasts with the form of heteroskedasticity discussed above, of which one representation used here is $Var(U_i) = k^2/n_i$. The conditions needed to establish Theil's result are reasonable. Individual behavior is modeled as independent draws from binomial populations. The probability of any individual using the HSL is allowed to vary with the individual. Grouping data into n_i-sized aggregations and employing the logit form leads to an aggregate error whose large sample variance is $k^2/n_i p_i(1-p_i)$. With 142 tract observations in our study, this large sample result seems relevant and will be tested.

Testing for heteroskedasticity proceeds by the Glejser method. Here, the absolute values of the OLS residuals are regressed against the suspected standard deviation of the error term. A significant "slope" coefficient indicates heteroskedasticity. See Johnston (1972: 220f) for details.

Should heteroskedasticity be present, use of the feasible Aitken estimator is indicated. This is easily accomplished by dividing all variables, including the dependent variable and the constant term, by the estimated standard deviation of the disturbance. In the case of the second type of heteroskedasticity, we of course use the $\hat{p}_i$ (estimated p_i), which is implicit in the OLS logit estimation, for both the (Glejser) testing of heteroskedasticity and the feasible Aitken estimation.

Using the Durbin Watson Statistic to Test for Omitted Explanatory Variables and Errors in Variables

First, the similarity between the omission of a variable and the commission of using an explanatory variable with error in it is demonstrated. Taking first the former case, suppose the population model is:

$$y = a + bz + cx + u.$$

The observed model, with omitted variable, is however:

$$y = a + cx + v \qquad \text{where } v = (u+bz).$$

Taking the latter case, suppose the true population model is:

$$y = a + b(x+z) + u.$$

But regressor is observed with error, the regression model used being:

$$y = a + bx + v \qquad \text{where } v = (u+bz).$$

The error terms in both cases are very similar, being the true disturbance plus a regressor or a part of a regressor (the part being the observation error). A relevant example of the latter would be the use of HSL or bus or car access plus line haul time, with omission of egress time—rather than using the total journey time. (Egress time is the time required to reach the final destination from the downtown HSL station or bus stop or parking lot.)

There is a simple method one can use in cross-section models to test for rather serious specification errors. Let z be the variable or the part of a variable we believe may be omitted from our regression equation, as above. Arrange the observations in ascending order of z—or a variable correlated with z (the stronger the rank order correlation the better). Calculate the Durbin Watson statistic. If z does belong in the model, then the Durbin Watson statistic will take on a small value under the above procedure. This is because the error in the misspecified model is of the form $v=(u+bz)$. Arranging the observations in order of z or a variable correlated with z will then tend to make successive differences of v small (hence the numerator of d small) relative to the total size of v (the denominator of d varying directly with this). Since the form of the "serial" correlation is not likely to follow an exact first order autoregressive scheme, use of the significance points for the d statistic should be regarded as approximative. This procedure has been employed successfully by Nerlove (1963), who found a serious omission in his specification of a cross-sectionally estimated cost function.

The power of the above test clearly depends on the following conditions: absence of countervailing "serial" correlation in u (an unlikely occurrence for the population error in a cross-section model), and bz being large enough relative to u so that the d statistic is made small. (Of course if bz is small relative to u, then we expect the coefficient biases to be small.) Further, if the observations are arranged in ascending order according to some variable w that is correlated with z (rather than according to the order of z itself), then the power of the test will also increase as the rank order correlation between w and z increases.

Testing for a Significantly Better Predictor

A way that can (and will) be used to decide whether one functional form is better than another is to test which is the better predictor. With a given set of data, one typically proceeds as follows. Fit each of the equations to a selected subset of the available data. Use the derived equations in deterministic form to yield a nonstochastic forecast of the dependent variable in the remaining observations (tracts). Calculate a summary statistic, typically the root mean square error (RMSE), in order to compare forecasts.

This is fine as far as it goes. But how can we tell if one prediction formula is significantly better than another? A smaller RMSE indicates that (on a squared error basis) formula one may be better than formula two, but how confident can we be that it would be better in repeated experiments?

Hoel (1947) made a first try at answering this question. The test that comes from his work is remarkably simple. Consider two forecasting formulas, f_1 and f_2, both trying to predict the expected value of y. Suppose we believe that f_1 is the correct or better predictor. To test this null hypothesis (against the alternative of accepting f_2 in place of f_1), we merely regress $(y - f_1)$ on $(f_2 - f_1)$ and a constant. If the "slope" coefficient is significantly positive, then f_1 is to be rejected in favor of f_2. If it is not significantly positive, then we cannot reject the null hypothesis at the test level of significance.

Williams and Kloot (see Williams [1959: 82]) followed up on Hoel's work, developing a more symmetrical test of two alternative forecasting formulas. Rather than assuming that one of the formulas will be favored from the outset, they test the null hypothesis that both predictors are equal in ability to forecast y. The resulting test is symmetrical in f_1 and f_2, as might have been anticipated. The test calls for doing a regression through the origin of $y-(1/2)$ (f_1+f_2) on (f_2-f_1). A significant positive coefficient indicates that f_2 is significantly better than f_1, while a significant negative coefficient indicates the opposite. An insignificant coefficient leaves the choice between f_1 and f_2 an undecided matter. To rank more than two alternative forecasting formulas, we merely do pairwise comparisons.

RESULTS OF THE DEMAND STUDY ON THE LINDENWOLD HSL

In this section, the results of extensive testing on the nature of demand for HSL use in 1970 are reported. First we discuss the variables found to significantly explain demand and then go on to econometric, policy, and other issues.

Explanatory Variables

The basic touchstones for determining whether to include a variable in the demand regression and which form of it to include are the sign and significance of the variable itself and the effect on the sign and significance of other variables in the equation.

The sign and degree of significance (or insignificance) of each of the independent variables showed great similarity across the four functional forms, as did their effects on the sign and significance of the rest of the explanatory variables. Accordingly, unless otherwise noted, the results discussed below should be taken as applying to all four functional forms: the linear, semilog, logit, and c logit with $c = 0.2$ (choice of compression ratios is discussed below). The variables will be discussed in the same order as they were above, to facilitate cross-reference to the discussion there.

Age, Sex, and Homeownership. The theoretical justification for including these variables is that they affect the utility function of the potential HSL users. Always significant at least at the 95 percent level is the sex variable, WORKER = (number of employed males aged sixteen years and over)/(total number of employed workers aged sixteen years and over). WORKER has the expected negative impact on p—indicating that, ceteris paribus, females tend to ride the HSL more than males. AGE22 = (number of persons age forty-five to sixty-four)/(number of persons aged twenty-five to forty-four) also has an inverse effect on p (older people are more averse to riding the HSL, perhaps because it involves more walking than use of a car would involve). This accords with the results of Lave (1970). However, neither it nor other age measures are terribly significant. While Kain (1964) finds that single family home dwellers are more likely to be auto users, ceteris paribus, than those living in multiple family or apartment units, this study finds absolutely no support for this contention in our New Jersey sample. A variable indicating the share of housing units that are single family, owner-occupied units has t tests consistently in the neighborhood of 0.

Auto Availability—The Person/Auto Ratio. PEWCAR = (total persons)/(total autos) is usually quite significant, though in the better specified models (which include a dummy variable for walk access), the t statistic of PEWCAR drops to about the 90 percent significance level. It always has the anticipated positive sign.

Income as a Separate Explanatory Variable—YMEDIN and Other Concepts. The census divides all households into two groups, families and unrelated individuals, and gives income data separately for each. YMEDIN is defined as a sort of weighted average of median family income and median unrelated individual income. Since median (as well as mean) income for the two groups is widely disparate and since the number of persons is the common denominator of the two, it was decided to use the number of persons literally in the denominator of YMEDIN. Also we divide the resulting quotient by 2,000 (approximately the number of working hours in a year) to derive a per capita income figure in dollars per hour. That is,

$$\text{YMEDIN} = \frac{\left(\begin{array}{c}\text{median in-}\\\text{come of}\\\text{families}\end{array}\right)\left(\begin{array}{c}\text{number of}\\\text{families}\end{array}\right) + \left(\begin{array}{c}\text{median in-}\\\text{come of un-}\\\text{related in-}\\\text{dividuals}\end{array}\right)\left(\begin{array}{c}\text{number of}\\\text{unrelated}\\\text{individuals}\end{array}\right)}{(\text{total number of persons}) \ (2{,}000)}$$

Four alternatives to YMEDIN were tried. First, YMEAN substitutes mean family income and mean unrelated individual income for the corresponding median figures. YMDIN1 and YMEAN1 are the same as YMEDIN and YMEAN respectively, except that instead of dividing by the number of persons, we divide by the number of (families + unrelated individuals). These give hourly household, rather than per capita, income figures. However, combining families and unrelated individuals in the denominator seems rather like combining apples and oranges. Some account should be taken, it would seem, of the fact that the larger family incomes must be split among more people. The fifth income concept, MEDALL, suffers from the same problem. MEDALL gives the median income of all families and unrelated individuals taken together as a group.

As expected YMEAN and YMEDIN do better than the other three concepts. Further, YMEDIN outperforms YMEAN somewhat.

YMEDIN is positively signed and quite significant in all regressions. The positive sign agrees with the CATS (1973) findings for Chicago and gives support for the primacy of the utility arguments over the cost arguments (see discussion on income, above).

Housing Costs and Supernumerary Income. To allow for households being in consumer's disequilibrium with respect to housing expenditures, SUPER, a supernumerary income (income after housing expenditures) measure, was tried in place of income. Overall, SUPER performs about as well as YMEDIN. It seems to perform a little worse than YMEDIN as a multiplier of time and a little better than YMEDIN as a divider of price; however, the regression equations are so similar and the results sufficiently mixed that no strong case can really be made. As for the fact that SUPER and YMEDIN perform about equally well overall, we must conclude that, at least in our case study, the disequilibrium problems mentioned previously are not serious. In further support of this conclusion, we note that separate housing cost and rental cost variables (EVHOME and ERENT, respectively) do not perform well; while they usually carry the correct sign, they are almost always insignificant.

Destination Variables. The census gives only broad indications of workplace destination. CBD1, CAMDN1, and PHILA1 are three destination variables indicating the fraction of potential users going to the Philadelphia CBD, Camden County (through the middle of which the HSL runs), and the rest of Philadelphia County (aside from the CBD). All three have the expected positive influence on p, though PHILA1 is not always significant at the 95 percent level (CBD1 and CAMDN1 always are). PHILA1 is much more significant in the nonlinear than in the linear equations, and this is taken as a plus point for the nonlinear equation forms, since we expect a priori that PHILA1 will be significantly positive.

Dummy Variable for Walk Access. The dummy variable for walk access, DUMMY, is always right signed and highly significant and makes a significant addition to the R^2 of the equation (of about 0.03 to 0.06).

Price and Time Variables. Price and time measurements are taken as originating from the centroid of each tract, a fairly innocuous procedure since the tracts are generally quite small. Trips are assumed to terminate, for purposes of these calculations, at the Philadelphia CBD (a place at or around which most trips do, in fact, end). The biasing effects that the absence of detailed destination data create are discussed and tested for below.

Many price and trip time concepts were tried. The conclusions are:

1. Time variables not multiplied by income or some function of income don't work at all (i.e., are insignificant and/or wrong signed). While it is generally accepted that the value of time (VOT) varies with income, rather than being constant across income levels, some studies still do not multiply time by a VOT expression.

2. Letting T_i be the time spent riding the ith mode (i=car, bus, HSL) and Y = income (median—see above), we find that variables of the form $T_i \cdot Y$, which posit that the value of time spent on the ith mode (VOT_i) is proportional to income, also do not work well.

3. A more complicated relation between the VOT_i and income is found to work exceedingly well; it is $VOT_i = (Y)(a_i + b_i Y)$. This allows the value of time fraction ($VOTF_i$) to vary with income, the $VOTF_i$ being the number that, when multiplied by income, gives the VOT for riding the ith mode. Note that here $VOTF_i = (a_i + b_i Y)$, a_i and b_i being estimated parameters.[6]

4. Other time expressions were tried. While the inverse relation $T_i(Y)$ $(a_i + b_i/Y)$ and the general U-shaped form $T_i(a_i + b_i Y + c_i Y^2)$ do not work as well as $T_i(Y)(a_i + b_i Y)$, it is found that $T_i(Y)(a_i + b_i Y^{1/2})$ works comparably well. The data and statistical procedures allow us to rule out some formulations as inferior, but are not good enough to decide between the more similar forms. A high degree of multicollinearity between the six time variables is the principle reason.

5. Using time differences in place of time levels is a vastly inferior specification. There is not a great deal of difference between using price differences and price levels.

The poor performance of time differences is undoubtedly due to the fact that the relevant constraints for using differences are far from being satisfied. That is, it seems intuitively reasonable that raising the price of the HSL by $x \not{c}$ might have about the same effect as lowering the price of all alternative modes by $x \not{c}$ (as in fact is found to be the case). It seems equally plausible that a similar result will not hold for the case of time— since a minute of HSL time carries with it very different amenities than a minute of car or bus time. The failure of time differences to be significant may also be construed as evidence for rejecting the hypothesis that the

---

[6] Here and occasionally elsewhere in this chapter, value of time (VOT) and value of time fraction (VOTF) expressions are derived on the basis of the assumption that the price terms are simply price levels, P_i. In fact, as discussed below, P_i/Y and $P_i/Y^{1/2}$ are found to be somewhat better choices. Using these two expressions instead of P_i, multiplies by Y and $Y^{1/2}$ both VOT_i and $VOTF_i$.

value of saving time on one mode is a weighted average of the value of saving time on the other two modes.

6. Price and time ratios work poorly. Even though the pathbreaking study of Warner (1962) used ratios, their use is now largely discredited at the theoretical level. (See above for compelling arguments against the use of ratios.) Empirically, ratio variables are found here to be insignificant and often wrong signed.

7. There has been some debate about whether trips become more or less arduous with the pure passage of time (or whether there is no change). For example, might the last ten minutes of a twenty minute journey be more or less arduous than the first ten minutes? To shed light on this, we replaced the usual time concept, $T_i(Y) (a + bY)$, by each of the following, in turn:

a. $T_i^{1/2}(Y) (a+bY)$
b. $T_i^{3/2}(Y) (a+bY)$
c. $T_i^2(Y) (a+bY)$

The results were that the variables using $T_i^{3/2}$ and T_i^2 were slightly more significant than those using T_i, and those using T_i were slightly more significant than those using $T_i^{1/2}$. Thus there is some tilt toward the increasing arduousness side; however, the differences are highly insignificant. We still must question whether past studies, which have generally assumed constant arduousness, were always employing the best premise.[7]

8. Aside from price ratios and differences, mentioned above, four price concepts are tried:

a. P_i
b. P_i/Y
c. $P_i/Y^{1/2}$
d. $P_i(a - bY)$

Concept (a) tests plain price levels, while (b) incorporates the idea that the price effect should diminish with rising income, as discussed previously. While (c) allows this diminishing price effect to occur more slowly,

---

[7] Also tried were the following increasing and decreasing arduousness variables:

d. $T_i^{1/2}$	g. $T_i^{1/2} \cdot Y$
e. $T_i^{3/2}$	h. $T_i^{3/2} \cdot Y$
f. T_i^2	i. $T_i^2 \cdot Y$

These variables were always wrong signed and/or insignificant, which indicates, as before, that the interaction of time with income is misspecified in these forms.

(d) tests for a price effect that falls linearly (rather than inversely) with income.

The results are that (a), (b), and (c) are all clearly superior to (d). Concept (b) is somewhat better than (a) and (c), judging from the fact that YMEDIN is most significant when (b) is used. As noted in the earlier discussion of the CATS (1973) study, incomplete allowance for income's effect on price (if such an effect is present) tends to make a separate positive income term insignificant. This is just what is observed here!

As noted in item 5 above, price differences may be substituted freely for price levels. The results here are the same in either case.

The Demand Equation of Choice. While there are many good ones,[8] perhaps the best demand equation of all those examined is equation (3.19). It is a c logit (with $c = 0.2$), estimated by ordinary least squares. All price and time variables are significant at the 95 percent level—except bus price, which is highly insignificant in this and all other regressions.[9] Additional summary data are included with the regression. (See facing page.)

This completes our results on which variables should enter the HSL demand function and on the way they should enter. Still, there are many more interesting and pertinent questions that are to be answered. These are taken up in the next section. The above equation foreshadows the results of many of the tests, such as that for the best regression equation, as well as those for heteroskedasticity and errors and omissions in the explanatory variables.

Further Results on Demand Estimation

The remaining important questions are listed below. Their answers follow, in the order in which the questions are asked.

1. What is the best ratio of the cost of hard time to easy time to schedule delay time for bus users? What is the best ratio of the cost of hard time to easy time for HSL users?

[8] A detailed set of equations as well as a variables key are reproduced in the author's dissertation. (The interested reader should consult Westley [1976: Appendix C].)

The highly insignificant variables could be pruned from this equation with no important effects on the remaining variables; however, they are left in for illustrative purposes.

[9] The insignificance of bus price (the only price or time concept to be insignificant in any of the better equation specifications) may well be due to a combination of collinearity between the three price variables (simple correlations run high) and to the comparative insignificance of the bus relative to the car as a competing mode for the HSL. Further, the money cost of the bus is generally a small part of the total trip costs, time costs being much more important. Under this reasoning, we might expect bus time costs to be more significant in the regressions than bus money costs, as is, in fact, observed.

Dependent variable: $\log\left(\dfrac{1-p}{p} - \dfrac{1-0.2}{0.2}\right)$ Mean of Dependent Variable: 3.27   (3.19)

(Mean of p = 0.0463)

Independent Variables	Estimated Coefficients	t Statistics	Mean of Independent Variables	Units of Independent Variables	Standard Deviation of Independent Variables
Constant	11.24	3.55	1.00	dimensionless	0
CBD1	-9.85	-2.60	0.051	number of persons ratio	0.030
PHILA1	-2.31	-1.39	0.187	number of persons ratio	0.065
CAMDN1	-2.53	-3.73	0.474	number of persons ratio	0.215
WORKER	6.92	2.42	0.646	number of persons ratio	0.048
YMEDIN	-4.44	-2.38	1.61	dollars per hour per person	0.396
AGE22	0.529	1.17	0.936	number of persons ratio	0.323
EVHOME	0.025	0.72	13.25	($1000s) (number of households ratio)	7.40
ERENT	0.011	1.50	33.20	(dollars per month) (number of households ratio)	26.65
PEWCAR	-0.311	-1.77	2.63	(persons)/(autos)	0.990
DUMMY	-1.09	-4.17	0.169	dimensionless	0.376
P_r/Y	0.049	2.96	52.75	(cents)/(dollars per hour per person)	18.86
P/Y	-0.061	-4.25	88.20	(cents)/(dollars per hour per person)	22.73
P_b/Y	0.0016	0.08	34.45	(cents)/(dollars per hour per person)	10.31
$T_r \cdot Y$	-0.100	-2.45	103.66	(minutes) (dollars per hour per person)	22.66
$T_a \cdot Y$	0.308	2.96	43.53	(minutes) (dollars per hour per person)	14.81
$T_b \cdot Y$	-0.063	-2.70	104.16	(minutes) (dollars per hour per person)	43.75
$T_r \cdot Y^2$	0.067	3.21	176.45	(minutes) (dollars per hour per person)^2	64.98
$T_a \cdot Y^2$	-0.196	-3.10	74.42	(minutes) (dollars per hour per person)^2	40.04
$T_b \cdot Y^2$	0.031	2.39	181.49	(minutes) (dollars per hour per person)^2	119.78

2. What is the direction of variation between the value of time fraction (VOTF) and income?
3. Does the Durbin Watson test indicate any omitted variables or errors in variables?
4. Is heteroskedasticity a significant problem?
5. Of the linear, logit, and c logit, what is (are) the best functional form(s) for the HSL demand equation?
6. What are the values of the own-price, cross-price, own-time, cross-time, income, and other elasticities?
7. What is the percentage effect on ridership of a one standard deviation change in each of the explanatory variables?

Time Aggregation. Many regressions were devoted to the task of trying to uncover relations between the different types of time. This was difficult because of the high degree of collinearity between the six disaggregated time variables. (The six variables are bus easy time, bus hard time, bus schedule delay time, HSL easy time, HSL hard time, car time.)

This multicollinearity problem is exacerbated by the fact that the time variables must be multiplied by income. Simple correlations between the six $T_i \cdot Y$ variables generally run around 0.6 or 0.7. Further, using what seem to be the best specifications, $(T_i)(Y)(a+bY)$, calls for twelve time variables and produces so much multicollinearity that the results are usually of little use. This problem is ultimately the motivation for aggregating time up to the modal level. We are somewhat in the position of being damned if you do and damned if you don't. If the seemingly correct specification is used, there is too much multicollinearity to derive many useful relations. If we avoid some of the multicollinearity by using the simple $T_i \cdot Y$ form, then we probably commit a specification error, which also leads to many silly results. An important compromise proved to be the use of $T_i \cdot Y^2$, which performs much better than $T_i \cdot Y$—indicating the strong variation of the VOTF with income. Because $T_i \cdot Y^2$ variables tended to be more often right signed and significant than $T_i \cdot Y$ variables, using them aided in the discovery of the relations between the cost of the various types of time.

The results of the many disaggregated time runs are, of course, quite varied. I summarize the results for three crucial ratios. The ratios sought are:

1. (cost of bus schedule delay time)/(cost of bus easy time)
2. (cost of bus hard time)/(cost of bus easy time)
3. (cost of HSL hard time)/(cost of HSL easy time).

The figures on ratio 1 vary mostly in the 0.20 to 0.50 range. One regression produced a whopping 2.08 ratio; otherwise the results were consistently less than 0.60. This accords well with our a priori notion that schedule delay time can often be used somewhat productively and hence its cost should be less than the cost of easy time. The figure selected for ratio 1 is 0.35; that is, to aggregate time up to the modal level, schedule delay time is given a weight of 0.35, compared with a weight of 1 for easy time.

The values of ratio 2 fall mostly in the range of 1.5 to 3.5. Occasional wild values are also obtained here (0.48, 0.82, 9.14). A value of 2.5 accords well with previous work and is used to weight bus hard time in this study. Values of ratio 3 are more varied than those in ratio 2, but in general are higher. A figure of 3.5 seems to be reasonable here.

While a large amount of prior information was used to guide our choices of ratio values, it is also true that results derived here tend to conform roughly to past patterns and hence support them. The most consistent ratio was undoubtedly ratio 1, many runs producing values within a small band about 0.35. This consistency is fortunate, since no prior work exists on the likely value of this ratio.

The VOTF. One of the seemingly more puzzling features of the demand equations is the exact quantitative character of the value of time fraction. The regression equation reproduced above is typical of the results.

In that equation, as well as over a wide range of different specifications of independent and dependent variables, we find that for incomes under about $1.50 the VOTF (and hence the VOT) is negative for HSL and auto users. For incomes over roughly $2.00, it is negative for bus users.[10] These are YMEDIN income numbers, and so they are measured as dollars per hour per person. Since the mean YMEDIN figure over all tracts is $1.61 (the standard deviation being 0.40), this says that for auto and HSL users with somewhat less than average income, riding to work is a leisure activity that is desirable in and of itself. For higher income people riding the bus, commuting is also, it seems, desirable. In such cases the more commuting the better—at least within the observed range of variation in time spent.

There are two seemingly puzzling aspects to the above results. The first is that the VOTF increases with income for HSL and auto users, while it decreases with income for bus users. The second is that the VOTF can be negative for some users. Why might such results be obtained?

Before answering these questions directly, it is well to note that bus users tend to be lower income people, while car and HSL users tend to be

---

[10] Recall that the value of time on a mode is obtained by dividing the coefficient of time by the coefficient of money cost for that mode.

higher income people. While no specific data are available to document this, it is clear that such is probably the case in view of the large time advantages that the car and HSL have over the bus. The car and HSL, further, are more expensive in money terms than the bus. Clearly, the rich will use the faster more expensive modes, while the poor will use the cheaper, slower mode. This much is surely intuitive and is backed by a large number of previous studies.

With a different economic and social strata of people using the different modes, it is perhaps not so surprising that the VOTF should fall with income in one case (bus) and rise with income in the other cases (car and HSL). It has been pointed out above that there is little real evidence on whether wage differentials precisely compensate for variations in the arduousness of work tasks. It may well be that in the kind of very low income jobs that low income bus users do, there is less than full compensation for unpleasantness, while in the comparatively higher paying jobs that the higher income bus users do, the compensation for unpleasantness is more complete, fully complete, or even overcomplete. As pointed out earlier, this pattern will result in the VOTF falling with increasing income, as is observed for bus users in the regressions. And the opposite pattern of compensation *cum* unpleasantness may prevail for relatively high and low wage earners within the higher income type jobs found in the world of the HSL and car commuters—resulting in the VOTF rising with income for HSL and car users.

One can also tell stories about different income strata within each modal commutation group being income or leisure preferrers, this resulting in the observed pattern of VOTF variations. Combinations of the institutional work week argument and the wage differentials argument are also possible. The paucity of prior empirical evidence and the failure of a priori reasoning to give us hard notions on the nature of VOTF make it difficult to know whether the VOTFs derived here are behaving as they should. This being the case, one might view the current findings as evidence to be compared with future studies.

While the above argument points to the possibility of accepting, at least on a tentative basis, the discovered directions of variation between VOTF and income, it is harder to accept these findings insofar as they lead to negative VOTFs. Before presenting the estimation problems that might have led to these seemingly strange results, it is well to observe that the results may not be as strange as they first seem.

First of all, we get negative VOTFs only for low income HSL and car users and for high income bus users. As already pointed out, HSL and car users will in general be of above average income, while bus users will generally be of below average income. Therefore, it is precisely the minority of those using each mode (especially the bus, where the VOTF is positive over an especially large range) who appear as having a negative VOTF. Having pointed out that those with a negative VOTF are a relatively small group, it might be suggested that in fact perhaps the VOTF really is negative for this group!

To see this, recall that for a broad class of activities, sometimes termed leisure activities, the value of reducing time spent on the activity is, in fact, negative. There are positive utility gains to be obtained from increasing time spent on such activities, though the limited amount of time available to us each day dictates a point at which even leisure activities should be terminated. (See DeSerpa [1971] for a good discussion of these and related points.) An example is that a relaxed meal is more satisfying than a hurried one. The same is true of a round of golf and so forth. The explanation for the negative VOTFs appearing in our study may then be that for the commuters involved, going to work is a form of leisure activity.

This notion tends to violate our habit-formed modes of thought about the value of transportation time saving. Many cost-benefit studies, for example, allow a VOT of perhaps $3.00 for every commuter hour a new rail facility saves, the figure of $3.00 being "taken from the literature." However, the literature from which this figure is taken has never really tested for the possibility of both negative and positive VOTs. What is being suggested here is that the evidence presented may in fact be representing the true situation. For some of the commuters in our New Jersey study, commuting may in fact be a leisure activity. The ramifications of this, if true, are enormous—especially in the area of cost-benefit analyses of new transport facilities, where time savings are often given the place of the primary benefit. Incidentally, I have no strong sociological or other reasons why low income HSL and car users and high income bus users should be the ones to regard commuting as leisure activities, but readers (especially sociologically minded ones) are invited to ponder the question and the ramifications of adducing the required strong reasons!

Of course, there are some possible statistical reasons for disregarding such results as we have here. On the basis of these, the possible existence of a negative VOTF may be denied, despite its consistent presence in the regression equations of this study.

One such reason is the high degree of multicollinearity that exists between the six time regressors $(T_a \cdot Y, T_b \cdot Y, T_r \cdot Y, T_a \cdot Y^2, T_b \cdot Y^2, T_r \cdot Y^2)$. This is certainly an impediment to correctly disentangling the influences of the various terms. While it cannot be stated for certain that a particular pattern of collinearity may not be causing some of our time regressors to take on the wrong sign, it is also true that all six of the time variable coefficients are statistically quite significant. Further, they retain their sign and significance under a wide variety of changes in the specifications of the dependent variable and of other explanatory variables. Further, when collinearity is reduced by regressing only three time variables of the form $T_i \cdot Y$, the coefficients of these three variables are usually only insignificantly different from 0. This result certainly is consistent with the subtler pattern of VOTF variation suggested here—that the VOTF is negative for some users and positive for others. In summary, while multicollinearity certainly is a problem, there is evidence suggesting that it really may not be behind the negative VOTFs obtained. But one other problem, potentially serious, still lurks in the background of this question.

Testing for Omitted Regressors and Errors in Variables. The other major set of objections to be raised against the demand study as it is done revolve around the idea that there may be important omitted regressors or errors in variables. Testing for this certainly is in order. The Durbin Watson test, described above, is employed here.

Perhaps the major such error is that egress time is basically not included (either as a separate variable or as part of overall time). The only exception to this is that five extra minutes are added to HSL walk time, based on egress considerations.[11]

Two possible relations may exist between the omitted egress time variables and the time measures actually used. The two may be functionally related, either negatively or positively, indicating that a longer access and line haul segment may be positively correlated with either a longer or shorter egress portion of the trip (the latter perhaps being more likely). Or the length of the egress portion of the trip may be essentially unrelated to the length of the rest of the work journey.

We test the first hypothesis (that a relation exists between omitted egress time and the time variables used) by first arranging the OLS errors in ascending order of TY=(car time) (YMEDIN) and then calculating the associated Durbin Watson (d) statistic. Car time is used because it is the only nonaggregated modal time variable and hence may be the most accurate. (HSL time includes easy and hard time; bus time includes these as well as schedule delay time.) But clearly, the time measures over different modes are highly correlated, and so the choice should not matter greatly. And because of the discovered high intercorrelations between time variables, car time should be correlated with the composite of omitted egress times, if there is the hypothesized relation between omitted and

---

[11] Since there are about seventy auto parking lots and garages in the one hundred square blocks of downtown Philadelphia, and since the bus makes a fairly complete set of loops through downtown, and since the HSL has only four Philadelphia stations, it seems clear that HSL users will have in general a longer walk to their workplace. Accordingly, five minutes of walking time are added for HSL users, as an adjustment for the egress portion of the trip.

included time concepts. YMEDIN, of course, acts as a correlate to a complex composite of first and second (and perhaps higher) order income terms. Since the amount of egress time omitted on each mode is not known, we cannot know the correct relative weights for the first and second order income terms; hence we use YMEDIN as a correlated proxy.

We test the second hypothesis (that egress times are essentially random with respect to included time measures) by arranging the OLS residuals in ascending order of YMEDIN or $(YMEDIN)^2$—both producing the same ordering—and then calculating the Durbin Watson d. As above, YMEDIN or $(YMEDIN)^2$ is a proxy for an unknown polynomial in YMEDIN.

Both hypotheses are tested on the residuals of a logit as well as a linear version of the regression equation reproduced above.[12]

Before reporting the results of these tests, it should be pointed out that other errors are undoubtedly present in our measures of time. For example, there are errors in our aggregation procedure for calculating total HSL and bus times. In addition, errors are undoubtedly made in deriving the disaggregated time estimates themselves. The reader may be able to think of other sources of error. But when the entirety of these errors are taken together (after being multiplied by income expressions) they are still either going to be related with the time measures used or they are going to be random with respect to these measures (and therefore likely correlated only with income). In sum, if omitted variables or errors in variables are indeed a significant problem (because the omitted variables really do play a significant role in helping to explain demand), one or more of the computed d statistics ought to have a low value. This, in fact, was my strong expectation at the time the computations were done.

The results were dramatic and stunning. The Durbin Watson statistics were:

1. logit run   —ordering residuals on TY: $DW = 2.09$
2. linear run   —ordering residuals on TY: $DW = 1.97$

3. logit run   —ordering residuals on YMEDIN: $DW = 2.17$

4. linear run   —ordering residuals on YMEDIN: $DW = 2.01$

---

[12] The logit is here and in many other cases the representative of all the nonlinear forms. It is selected because it is more realistic than the semilog and less arbitrary than the c logit. The reader should be aware, however, that the criteria and tests described below will be the final touchstones for deciding which functional form should be used in any given situation. The use of the logit as a representative is only a matter of convenience, in view of the large computational burden.

No "serial correlation," and therefore no significant errors or omissions in time variables, are detected at least insofar as they are correlated with YMEDIN and *TY*. The *d* statistics are so close to 2 that the refutation is quite convincing. In sum, it seems as though negative VOTFs may, in fact, be the order of the day for some New Jersey commuters.

Heteroskedasticity. We employ the Glejser (1969) test for heteroskedasticity—in which the absolute values of OLS residuals are regressed against a postulated form for the standard deviation of the population error term. As discussed earlier, two equations for the error variance are tried:

$$Var(U_i) = k^2/n_i \tag{3.20}$$
$$Var(U_i) = k^2/n_i\hat{p}_i(1-\hat{p}_i) \tag{3.21}$$

where U_i = error in the ith tract
n_i = number of potential users in the ith tract
$\hat{p}_i$ = OLS estimated fraction of potential users riding the HSL in the ith tract
k = a constant.

The Glejser test consistently rejects heteroskedasticity of equation (3.20); it cannot reject at even the 99+ percent significance level equation (3.21) in the logit regressions. While heteroskedasticity is significantly present, it is not of great importance. This can be seen by the fact that the R^2 in the Glejser regression never rises above 0.1 and, more importantly, by the fact that reestimation of the logit regressions using the feasible Aitken method results in little change in the size of the coefficients or their significances. Further, what changes there are are mixed: some variables become more significant while others become less significant. We would expect more efficient estimation and hence higher t statistics had we discovered serious heteroskedasticity.

Choosing the Best Functional Form—Prediction Tests. Based on our a priori notions of which variables should be significant and what the direction of their impact on HSL ridership should be, it is difficult to choose between the three basic functional forms—linear, logit, and c logit with $c=0.2$.

A compression ratio of 0.2 has been used in the c logit because it is found that, uniformly, the lower the value of c the better the regression equation. Using the explanatory variable list shown in the regression equation reproduced above and values of c equal to 0.2, 0.3, 0.4, 0.5, 0.6, 0.7, 0.8, and 0.9, it is found that smaller c values result in more significant

t statistics for virtually all independent variables and also result in ever lower sums of squared errors in explaining p. Not only does the equation with $c=0.2$ have the best statistical properties, but its use in the prediction tests allows one to differentiate the c logit as much as possible from the logit. And $c=0.2$ is almost the minimum value of c that is possible to use, since the reported p in one tract is 0.189.

The semilog regression equations were almost identical to those of the logit and so do not warrant separate consideration.[13] The logit rather than the semilog was retained because it seems a priori the superior functional form.

Computing the R^2 of the three forms on a comparable basis—namely, based on their ability to explain p (the fraction of potential users that are HSL commuters)—yields an interesting comparison. The results of doing this over the 142 observation sample period are shown below for linear, logit, and c logit (with $c=0.2$) runs, each with the same independent variables shown in the regression equation reproduced above. This explanatory variable list is considered the best for all three functional forms.

logit R^2 = 0.6598
linear R^2 = 0.7361
c logit R^2 = 0.7692

While this provides some evidence in favor of the c logit and against the ordinary logit, a more conclusive set of tests involves testing which equation can best be used to predict demand in tracts that are outside the sample points used for fitting. This is of great relevance, since we want our estimated demand relation to be transportable across space (i.e., as relevant as possible for other cities). In addition, the ability to forecast properly is the acid test of the validity of a behavioral relation. Within the sample period errors can be largely masked by the minimum squared error fitting process, but in a good prediction test, a model's shortcomings should stand out in naked relief.

In all, four different prediction tests are carried out. In each of them, demand equations of the three forms used above in the R^2 test are reestimated on a subset of tracts (either thirty-three or sixty-six tracts). The fitted relations are used to predict demand in the rest of the tracts. Comparisons of RMSE are then made, and the Williams-Kloot test is employed to determine if one functional form is forecasting significantly better than another. In addition to comparisons of three basic models, a

---

[13] This is because in the vast bulk of the tracts p is less than 0.10 and in a solid majority it is less than 0.05. As a result, $log(p)$ will not differ much from $log\ [p/(1-p)]$.

"naive" or simple forecasting model is added and compared with the others. The naive model is a simple fitted linear equation of the form:

$$p = a + b (P_r - P_a) + c(T_r - T_a) \tag{3.22}$$

That is, demand for the HSL is related to the relative time and cost advantages of the HSL over its largest competitor, the auto. In the sample period fit b and c are significant and have the expected signs, and the R^2 of the equation is 0.4500. Hence, this seems a reasonably good choice of simple or naive models. Like the other three equations, this naive model will be reestimated over the same thirty-three or sixty-six tracts, and the resulting relation will be used to forecast demand for the rest of the tracts. Its predictions will be ranked along with the rest.

The first two tests involve using for the sample period of fit the thirty-three and then the sixty-six tracts with highest estimated percentage HSL usage rates, according to the c logit equation reproduced above. That is, tracts are ranked according to their $\hat{p}$ values (or equally, according to their $\log \left(\dfrac{1 - p}{p} - \dfrac{1 - 0.2}{0.2} \right)$ values) and those with the highest thirty-three (then sixty-six) $\hat{p}$ values are used to estimate the four forecasting formulas. We truncate the sample according to $\hat{p}$ (and hence according to a linear combination of the explanatory variables) instead of p, the actual HSL usage rates, because of the well known result that OLS is biased under the latter procedure. The selection of tracts is not greatly different whether we use $\hat{p}$ or p.

These are the best, or at least toughest, two tests of the four that are employed. Not only do we use a forecasting formula to predict usage in tracts outside the sample points of fit, but we allow the fitting process to be done only over a part of the range of the p values. Recall from the earlier discussion that one of the main behavioral differences between the linear and nonlinear models is the relative effect on high and low use tracts of a given change in an independent variable. By fitting the four relations only to high use tract data, we test whether the derived impact coefficients of the explanatory variables are more reasonable in the linear or nonlinear cases. We do this by comparing how the high-use-tract-fitted formulas forecast in low use tracts and, hence, derive a fairly direct test of a fundamental difference in behavioral implications between the linear and nonlinear models.

In addition, these two prediction tests have the advantage of simulating a frequently encountered, real world situation. Often the first rail line built in a metropolitan area is located in a very high use corridor. After that, other rail lines are put in lower use corridors, or the initial line is extended further out into more rural, lower use areas. (Both of these possibilities are being considered, in fact, in Philadelphia—for the case of the HSL.) It is desirable that fitted demand relations based on the experience and data garnered from the operation of the first high use corridor rail line be capable of being applied in predicting demand on the newly proposed lower use rail lines. It is therefore of importance to know which demand equations are best at doing this. The first two hypothesis tests will provide evidence on this question.

The second pair of hypothesis tests use a stratified random sample of thirty-three and sixty-six tracts for sample period estimation, stratification being done again by estimated usage rates. Specifically, in the first of these tests, a random sample (drawn by lot) of eight of the thirty-three highest estimated use tracts, eight of the thirty-three second highest estimated use tracts, and seventeen of the lowest estimated use tracts is made. These sampling rates correspond to the proportion of the sampled subpopulations in the entire population. In the second of the tests (involving sixty-six stratified random tracts) samples are fifteen, fifteen, and thirty-six respectively. A stratified random sample is used rather than a pure random sample in order to insure greater heterogeneity of $\hat{p}$ (and hence p) values. This gives greater power to the test of which functional form predicts best after being fit on a heterogeneous sample of tracts.

The results of the four prediction tests are shown in Tables 3–1 and 3–2. Table 3–1 shows RMS forecasting errors, as well as sample period

Table 3–1. Prediction Tests—RMS Errors and Model Rankings.

	Linear	Naive	Logit	c Logit (c=0.2)
Test 1 Fit on the 33 highest use tracts	0.06823	0.05151	0.02893	0.02817
Ranking: c logit, logit, naive, linear				
Test 2 Fit on the 66 highest use tracts	0.06655	0.03629	0.01528	0.01583
Ranking: logit, c logit, naive, linear				
Test 3 Fit on 33 random tracts	0.05187	0.04124	0.07325	0.05733
Ranking: naive, linear, c logit, logit				
Test 4 Fit on 66 random tracts	0.02705	0.03580	0.04175	0.02782
Ranking: linear, c logit, naive, logit				
Sample Period Fit On all 142 tracts	0.02376	0.03430	0.02698	0.02222
Ranking: c logit, linear, logit, naive				

Table 3-2. Prediction—Williams-Kloot Tests of Significance.[a]

	Linear (+) versus Naive (−)	Linear (+) versus Logit (−)	Linear (+) versus c Logit (−)	Naive (+) versus Logit (−)	Naive (+) versus c Logit (−)	Logit (+) versus c Logit (−)
Test 1 Fit on the 33 highest use tracts	naive (−2.97)	logit (−11.15)	c logit (−14.25)	logit (−8.78)	c logit (−7.07)	no winner—leaning to c logit (−0.52)
Ranking: c logit then logit, naive, linear						
Test 2 Fit on the 66 highest use tracts	naive (−6.41)	logit (−20.89)	c logit (−23.37)	logit (−8.73)	c logit (−8.05)	no winner—leaning to logit (−0.86)
Ranking: logit then c logit, naive, linear						
Test 3 Fit on 33 random tracts	naive (−3.25)	linear (5.76)	linear (2.27)	naive (7.26)	naive (4.67)	c logit (−8.31)
Ranking: naive, linear, c logit, logit						
Test 4 Fit on 66 random tracts	linear (3.06)	linear (4.90)	no winner—leaning to linear (0.61)	no winner—leaning to naive (1.34)	c logit (−2.60)	c logit (−5.87)
Ranking: linear then c logit, naive then logit						

[a] t statistics shown in parentheses.

RMS errors. Table 3–2 shows the results of the Williams-Kloot tests—indicating the "winners" in each pair of comparisons and the associated Williams-Kloot t statistics. In both tables, the ranking of functional forms (from best to worst) is shown for each prediction test. In Table 3–2, an insignificant (at the 95 percent level) advantage of model a over model b is indicated in the ranking list by writing "a then b" rather than "a,b"—the latter indicating that model a is a significantly better predictor than model b.

We derive the following conclusions from these results. Explanations follow.

Conclusions:
1. C logit generally outperforms logit, dominating it in the random tract tests, and doing equally as well in the truncated sample tests.
2. C logit and logit outperform linear and naive when the fit is on high use tracts. When the fit is on stratified random tracts, the linear models outperform the logit and c logit, though in the sixty-six random tracts test, c logit beats naive and is only insignificantly worse than the linear model.
3. The RMS errors decline a great deal in the linear and naive models as we go from the high use tract fits to the random tract fits, while these errors roughly double for the logit and c logit.

Explanations:
1. This is a sensible result, since a great many people can be on the edge of indecision at aggregate tract usage rates of much less than 50 percent. The c logit here employs an indecision edge of 10 percent; this edge may in fact be lower (given especially the relatively few tracts with usage rates of 10 percent or more), but we are constrained by the fact that maximum usage is 18.9 percent in one tract. (We could try throwing out the high use tracts and compressing the logit further, though we pay a price in not being able to extrapolate up to very high usage rates. We also throw away some of our statistically most important observations.)
2. The highly nonlinear parts of the logit and c logit occur here at relatively high usage rates. The lesson is: only when there are sufficient observations on this nonlinear segment will the c logit and logit be improvements over the linear (and naive linear) models. But once we have sufficient high use observations, the logit and c logit appear to be the best models.

The number of observations on the sixty-six highest use tracts are: sixteen in test 3 and thirty in test 4. (It is, of course, thirty-three and sixty-six, respectively, in tests 1 and 2.) Note that while we add only three high use tracts in going from test 4 to test 1, the c logit goes from an insignificant loser to a significant winner over the linear. We must conclude that the low usage observations in test 4 have helped greatly to "keep the linear form honest." This reflects the poor assumptions behind the linear model—namely, that both high and low use tracts are equally on the edge of indifference as far as riding the HSL goes. The prediction tests here show this assumption to be false, the linear doing very badly when fitted only to high use tracts; it needs the averaging effects of being fitted to high and low use tracts in order to perform more reasonably.

In sum, the nonlinear forms should certainly be used when data only on comparatively high use tracts are available and the task is to predict demand in comparatively lower use tracts. The linear model should only be used if there are data on a broad range of usage rates with so few observations on high use tracts that the c logit could not be expected to be fitted accurately. In the present study, when there are around thirty or more high use tracts (here, having usage rates of approximately 3.5 percent or more), the c logit and linear seem to do about equally well in the random tract test, and so the c logit may be used here as well.

3. This accords with Conclusion 2: we need the low as well as the high use observations for the linear model to predict well (it can interpolate pretty well—cannot extrapolate); whereas the high use tract observations are the most important in fitting the logit and c logit. To see this last point, note that for the logit and c logit, the RMSE is roughly the same in test 1, with thirty-three of the highest use tracts, and test 4, with fifteen of the highest use tracts, fifteen of the second highest use tracts, and thirty-six of the lowest use tracts.

Further Notes:

Comparing tests 1 versus 2 and 3 versus 4—to see the effect of fitting the relation with more data—we see that doubling the number of observations used for fitting approximately cuts the RMSE of prediction in half. The only exceptions are for the naive model in tests 3 and 4, where the drop in RMS error is only about 15 percent instead of 50 percent, and for the linear model in tests 1 and 2 where the decline is negligible. This is probably related only to the particular samples chosen—very favorable to the naive model in 3 and/or unfavorable in 4, and very favorable to the linear model in 1 and/or unfavorable in 2.

In summary, the reasoning given earlier espousing the behavioral content of the nonlinear models over the linear seems dramatically confirmed by tests 1 and 2. The c logit emerges as perhaps the best overall functional form, subject to the very intuitive limitation that sufficient observations (perhaps thirty or more) on its nonlinear range be present before it is used.

Numerical Results—Percentage Effects of a One Standard Deviation Change in Each of the Independent Variables and Associated Elasticities. The usefulness of calculating elasticity type measures for explanatory variables, especially policy variables, is well known. They give managers and planners information on the likely effects on line ridership of raising rail fares by x percent, of cutting journey time by y percent, and so forth. Calculating the elasticities for such variables as age, sex, income, and the like may seem much less useful, since these variables do not appear to be under the control of the rail planner or manager. This is certainly true once the path of the rail line has been chosen. But since this book is examining precisely the question of where the line should be located, all these demographic and economic variables come under the control of the planner in the sense that he or she can choose the path of the line so as to manipulate the characteristics of those who fall in the passenger shed. It then becomes relevant to ask what the effect of altering these variables is. It also becomes relevant to ask how much real world variation in variables representing such concepts as age, sex, and the like there is likely to be. Because of these considerations, a calculation of the effect of a one standard deviation change in each of the independent variables is very useful. Results are presented in Table 3–3 for the case of regression equation (3.19).

Percentage effects on p (at its mean value of 0.0463) are given for a one standard deviation change up and down in each of the independent variables. The associated elasticity measures are also indicated. All calculations are done at the mean values, whenever a question of the choice of level arises. The only exceptions are the income levels assumed in calculating the last five impacts in Table 3–3. Higher than average incomes are used for HSL and auto users, while lower than average income is used in the bus case. This is done to adhere more closely to what the average income of the group at hand probably is. Calculations for bus price are omitted because this variable is wrong signed.

The results speak largely for themselves, and so comments will be fairly limited. We are mainly interested in Columns (2) and (5)—the percentage effects—for the nontime and nonprice variables (such as age, sex, etc.) and in Columns (4) and (6)—the elasticities—for the time and price variables. This is because planners have little power to change the first group of variables (age, sex, etc.). They can only alter the location of the rail line to better take advantage of the existing spatial patterns in these variables. A small percentage change in this type of independent variable may have a large percentage impact on ridership (i.e., a large elasticity), but the existing range of variation may be so small that little advantage can be taken of the high elasticity. An excellent example of this in the case at hand is the variable WORKER, which represents the

Table 3-3. Impact Measures.

(1) Independent Variable	(2) Percentage Effect on p of a One Standard Deviation Rise in the Independent Variable (Measured at mean of p)	(3) Standard Deviation of the Independent Variable as a Percentage of Its Mean	(4) Elasticity Associated with the Change in Column (2)—this = (2) ÷ (3).	(5) Percentage Effect on p of a One Standard Deviation Fall in the Independent Variable (Measured at mean of p)	(6) Elasticity Associated with the Change in Column (5)—this = (5) ÷ (3).
CBD1	24.6	59.68	0.41	-21.0	-0.35
PHILA1	12.0	34.65	0.35	-11.1	-0.32
CAMDN1	47.6	45.39	1.05	-35.7	-0.79
WORKER	-23.3	7.48	-3.12	27.9	3.73
AGE22	-12.5	34.49	-0.36	13.7	0.40
EVHOME	-13.7	55.81	-0.25	15.2	0.27
ERENT	-20.4	80.27	-0.25	23.8	0.30
PEWCAR	25.6	37.70	0.68	-21.7	-0.58
DUMMY	34.8	222.54	0.16	-28.0	-0.13
YMEDIN (total effect at Y=1.6)	27.3	24.58	1.11	-45.7	-1.86
HSL Price (at Y=2.0)	-36.8	28.57	-1.29	49.5	1.73
Car Price (at Y=2.0)	71.6	18.86	3.80	-47.8	-2.53
Bus Time (at Y=1.2)	51.5	29.90	1.72	-37.9	-1.27
HSL Time (at Y=2.0)	-41.2	14.58	-2.83	57.9	3.97
Car Time (at Y=2.0)	111.3	26.01	4.28	-62.6	-2.41

percentage of workers who are male. Here the elasticity is very large, but the range of variation (measured by the ratio of the standard deviation to the mean) is so small that the effect of a one standard deviation change in WORKER is to alter p by only about 25 percent, a fairly ordinary sized effect for the nontime and nonprice variables in the case at hand. Larger effects are found for CAMDN1, DUMMY, and YMEDIN.

We are more interested in the elasticity measures for the price and time (at least the HSL price and time) variables, because the planner has some control over them. Because the existing pattern of variation in such variables is not taken as given, we are more interested in finding out the impact on p of a calculated and controlled policy change. Of course, to the extent that we cannot influence price and time costs for the auto and bus, we then are interested exclusively in altering the path of the rail line to take best advantage of these patterns as they exist. Under such circumstances Columns (2) and (5)—the percentage effects—are of interest for the time and money costs by auto and bus.

As for changes in price and time that increase ridership we find the following elasticities:

HSL Price: 1.73
Auto Price: 3.80
Bus Time: 1.72
HSL Time: 3.97
Auto Time: 4.28

The figures support the notion that modal competition in New Jersey is very strong: small changes in costs have fairly large effects. These elasticities are greater than those of Lave (1970) for rail and McGillivray (1970) for bus. They are more in line with the elasticities found in Quarmby's (1967) analysis of buses in Leeds, England. We shall not dwell on these comparisons, but rather pass on to the heart of the matter at hand—optimal rail line mathematics and the application of this mathematics to solving the location problem. This is the subject matter of the next two chapters.

BIBLIOGRAPHY FOR CHAPTER 3

Allen, W. Bruce. 1970. "A Literature Search on Behavioral Modal Split." Regional Science Department, University of Pennsylvania. Unpublished.

American Automobile Association. 1971. *The Lindenwold Line*. Washington, D.C.

Becker, G. 1965. "A Theory of the Allocation of Time." *Economic Journal*, pp. 493–517.

Beesley, M.E. 1965. "The Value of Time Spent in Travelling: Some New Evidence." *Economica*, pp. 174–85.

Blackburn, A.J. 1970a. "A Nonlinear Model of the Demand for Travel." In R.E. Quandt, ed., *The Demand for Travel: Theory and Measurement*. Lexington, Mass.: D.C. Heath and Company.

————. 1970b. "An Alternative Approach to Aggregation and Estimation in the Nonlinear Model." In R.E. Quandt, ed., *The Demand for Travel: Theory and Measurement*. Lexington, Mass.: D.C. Heath and Company.

Brady, C.R., and M.J. Betz. 1971. "An Evaluation of Regression Analysis and the Gravity Model in the Phoenix Urban Area." *Journal of Transport Economics and Policy*, pp. 76–90.

Boyce, D., and W.B. Allen. 1972. "Interim Report" (for the Urban Mass Transportation Administration). Xerox.

Boyce, D.; K. Nguyen; T. Noyelle; and V. Vuchic. 1975. "Impact of Rapid Transit on Fuel Consumption and Cost for the Journey to Work." Unpublished.

CATS (Chicago Area Transportation Study). 1973. "Disaggregated Mode Choice Models of Downtown Trips in the Chicago Region." Technical report prepared by Martha Wigner. Offset.

Cesario, F.J. 1973. "A Generalized Trip Distribution Model." *Journal of Regional Science*, pp. 233–47.

deDonnea, F.X. 1972. "Cost-Benefit Analysis and the Evaluation of Non-Working Travel Time Savings: Some Question Marks." *Recherches Economiques de Louvain*, pp. 331–39.

DeSerpa, A.C. 1971. "A Theory of the Economics of Time." *Economic Journal*, pp. 828–46.

Fletcher, D.P.C. 1972. "The Peak in Road Passenger Transport." *Journal of Transport Economics and Policy*, pp. 211–12.

Foster, C.D., and M.E. Beesley. 1963. "Estimating the Social Benefit of Constructing an Underground Railway in London." *Royal Statistical Society Journal*, pp. 46–93.

Galbraith, K. 1969. *The Affluent Society*. 2nd ed. New York: Mentor.

Glejser, H. 1969. "A New Test for Heteroskedasticity," *Journal of the American Statistical Association*, pp. 316–23.

Goldberg. 1963. *Traffic in Towns*. London: HMSO.

Gordon, I.R., and S.L. Edwards. 1973. "Holiday Trip Generations." *Journal of Transport Economics and Policy*, pp. 153–68.

Gronau, R. 1970. "The Effect of Travelling Time on the Demand for Passenger Transportation." *Journal of Political Economy*, pp. 377–94.

Gronau, R., and R.E. Alcaly. 1969. "The Demand for Abstract Transport Modes: Some Misgivings." *Journal of Regional Science*, pp. 153–57.

Harrison, A.J., and D.A. Quarmby. 1969. "The Value of Time in Transport Planning: a Review." In *Theoretical and Practical Research on an Estimation of Time-Saving*. European Conference of Ministers of Transports, Report of the Sixth Round Table. Paris: Economic Research Center.

Hoel, P.G. 1947. "On the Choice of Forecasting Formulas." *Journal of the American Statistical Association*, pp. 605–11.

Howrey, E.P. 1969. "On the Choice of Forecasting Models for Air Travel." *Journal of Regional Science*, pp. 215–24.

Johnson, M. 1966. "Travel Time and the Price of Leisure." *Western Economic Journal*, pp. 135–45.

Johnston, J. 1972. *Econometric Methods*. New York: McGraw-Hill.

Jones, I.S. 1970. "Gravity Models and Generated Traffic." *Journal of Transport Economics and Policy*, pp. 208–11.

Kain, J.F. 1964. "A Contribution to the Urban Transportation Debate: An Econometric Model of Urban Residential and Travel Behavior." *Review of Economics and Statistics*, pp. 55–64.

———. 1967. "Postwar Metropolitan Development: Housing Preferences and Auto Ownership." *American Economic Review*, pp. 223–34.

Lancaster, K.J. 1966. "A New Approach to Consumer Theory." *Journal of Political Economy*, pp. 132–57.

Lang, A.S., and R.M. Soberman. 1964. *Urban Rail Transit: Its Economics and Technology*. Cambridge, Mass.: M.I.T. Press.

Lave, C.A. 1970. "The Demand for Urban Mass Transportation." *Review of Economics and Statistics*, pp. 320–24.

Lave, L.B. 1972. "The Demand for Intercity Passenger Transportation." *Journal of Regional Science*, pp. 71–84.

Lee, N., and M.Q. Dalvi. 1969. "Variations in the Value of Travel Time." *Manchester School of Economic and Social Studies*, pp. 213–36.

———. 1971. "Variations in the Value of Travel Time: Further Analysis." *The Manchester School of Economic and Social Studies*, pp. 187–204.

Lisco, T. 1967. "The Value of Commuter's Travel Time: A Study in Urban Transportation." Ph.D. dissertation, Department of Economics, University of Chicago.

Lövemark, O. 1972. "New Approaches to Pedestrian Problems." *Journal of Transport Economics and Policy*, pp. 3–9.

Mayberry, J.P. 1970. "Structural Requirements for Abstract-Mode Models of Passenger Transportation." In R.E. Quandt, ed., *The Demand for Travel: Theory and Measurement*. Lexington, Mass.: D.C. Heath and Company.

McDonough, C.C. 1973. "The Demand for Commuter Rail Transport." *Journal of Transport Economics and Policy*, pp. 134–43.

McGillivray, R.G. 1970. "Demand and Choice Models of Modal Split." *Journal of Transport Economics and Policy*, pp. 192–207.

McKay, R.V. 1973. "Commuting Patterns of Inner-City Residents." *Monthly Labor Review*, pp. 43–48.

Moses, L.N., and H.F. Williamson Jr. 1963. "Value of Time, Choice of Mode, and the Subsidy Issue in Urban Transportation." *Journal of Political Economy*, pp. 247–64.

Nerlove, M. 1963. "Returns to Scale in Electricity Supply." In C.F. Christ et al., *Measurement in Economics: Studies in Memory of Yehuda Grunfeld*. Stanford, Calif.: Stanford University Press.

Oort, C.J. 1969. "The Evaluation of Traveling Time." *Journal of Transport Economics and Policy*, pp. 279–86.

Pratt, R. 1970. "A Utilitarian Theory of Travel Model Choice." Paper presented at the 48th meeting of the Highway Research Board, Washington, D.C., January.

Quandt, R.E. 1968. "Estimation of Modal Splits." *Transportation Research,* pp. 41–50.

Quandt, R.E., and W.J. Baumol. 1966. "The Demand for Abstract Transport Modes: Theory and Measurement." *Journal of Regional Science*, pp. 13–26.

———. 1969. "The Demand for Abstract Transport Modes: Some Hopes." *Journal of Regional Science*, pp. 159–62.

Quandt, R.E., and K.H. Young. 1969. "Cross-Sectional Travel Demand Models: Estimates and Tests." *Journal of Regional Science*, pp. 210–14.

Quarmby, D.A. 1967. "Choice of Travel Mode for the Journey to Work: Some Findings." *Journal of Transport Economics and Policy*, pp. 273–314.

Starkie, D.N.M. 1971. "Modal Split and the Value of Time." *Journal of Transport Economics and Policy*, pp. 216–20.

Theil, H. 1971. *Principles of Econometrics.* New York: John Wiley and Sons Inc.

Thomas, T.C. 1968. "Value of Time for Commuting Motorists." Stanford Research Institute Report. *Highway Research Board*, January.

U.S. Department of Transportation, Bureau of Public Roads. 1964. *Traffic Assignment Manual.* Washington, D.C.

———. 1965. *Calibrating and Testing a Gravity Model for any Size Urban Area.* Washington, D.C.

———. 1966. *Modal Split.* Washington, D.C.

———. 1967. *Guidelines for Trip Generation Analysis.* Washington, D.C.

Vickerman, R. 1972. "The Demand for Non-Work Travel." *Journal of Transport Economics and Policy*, pp. 176–210.

Vigrass, J.W. 1972. "The Lindenwold Hi–Speed Transit Line." *Railway Management Review*, pp. 28–52.

Warner, S. 1962. *Stochastic Choice of Mode in Urban Travel: A Study in Binary Choice.* Evanston, Ill.: Northwestern University Press.

Westley, G. 1976. "The Optimal Location of Urban Radial Rail Lines." Ph.D. dissertation, University of Pennsylvania.

Williams, E.J. 1959. *Regression Analysis.* New York: John Wiley.

Wilson, A.G. 1967. "A Statistical Theory of Spatial Distribution Models." *Transportation Research*, pp. 253–69.

Wootan, M.J., and G.W. Pick. 1967. "A Model for Trips Generated by Households." *Journal of Transport Economics and Policy*, pp. 137–53.

Young, K.H. 1972. "A Synthesis of Time-Series and Cross-Section Analyses: Demand for Air Transportation Services." *Journal of the American Statistical Association*, pp. 560–66.

※ *Chapter 4*

Optimal Rail Location:
Basic Analysis

INTRODUCTION

By discussing the benefits and costs of a line and the functional form for demand, the work of the previous two chapters has set the stage for the unfolding of the optimal rail line location techniques. This chapter discusses selection of the revenue-maximizing rail line, developing what will be a methodology basic to finding the full welfare-maximizing line. For further illustration, the next chapter looks at two more of the most important terms in the benefit-cost expression—congestion and right of way land costs—and discusses how these should be incorporated in the optimization methodology. Other important topics, such as optimization under constraints, are also examined in the next chapter.

The work of the present chapter is divided into two parts, corresponding to two different assumptions on the nature of the path commuters will take to gain access to the line. The two path types are called the vertical access and the least total cost access paths and are discussed in turn in the next sections. While many other access assumptions could have been made (e.g., radial-circumferential, grid street, grid street with diagonals, etc.), the large number of such cases necessitates that some choice be made among them. The two chosen are felt to be highly applicable in the urban-suburban context, as well as representative of the possibilities, one being a fixed rule (vertical access) and the other being a behavioral rule (least total cost access). Further, by using distance markup factors (discussed below), these two schemes can probably be used with reasonable accuracy in all the access cases noted above.

GENERAL CONSIDERATIONS FOR ANY
ACCESS SCHEME

The starting point for discussion is a rail demand function of the type discussed in Chapter 3. This gives the rail use share out of total potential users as a function of tract-specific characteristics as well as the time and money costs of the rail line and alternative modes.[1] Of particular importance are the time and money costs of using the rail line, for it is these that vary with a change in line location.[2] A review of the components of rail cost (access cost, line haul cost, walking and waiting time, rail station parking cost, egress costs), such as contained in Chapter 3, is enough to verify that total rail trip costs (money plus time and amenities—insofar as the last is captured by the mode-specific time coefficient) for the jth tract can be written in the form:

$$L_j = C_{0j} + (C_{1j}) \text{ (access distance)} + (C_{2j}) \text{ (line haul distance)} \qquad (4-1)$$

where C_{1j} is the per mile access cost from the jth tract and C_{2j} is the per mile line haul cost from the jth tract.

Contained within the $[C_{1j}$ (access distance)] term are time (plus amenity) and money access costs. Under the usual assumptions of fixed (or tract varying) per mile driving cost, a given access speed—which may vary with the tract, some line path invariant assumption on the share of line users in each tract that will be kiss-n-riders, pay parkers, and free parkers, and known income and other characteristics in the jth tract—we get per mile access costs as C_{1j}. While we assume these costs vary only with the origin tract (j), we may wish to generalize this assumption to allow, for example, access speed (hence access costs) to vary not only with origin tract but also with the point of access on the rail line. We would then have to construct a set of two dimensional speed gradients, one for each tract. Denoting the equation of the rail line as $y = f(x)$, the speed from the jth tract to the point of access, $(x_a, f(x_a))$, would be $s_i(x_a, f(x_a))$. This refinement does not seem to be worth the trouble, and is not pursued here.

---

[1] Amenity costs are, as discussed in Chapter 3, included in time costs.

[2] Time and money costs of using the car and bus may also fall somewhat because of the reduced street congestion that accompanies a new line. While such savings may be important in the aggregate, the reduction in costs for any one motorist or bus user is generally quite small—well within the margin of statistical error of estimating the demand relation. (For example, Foster and Beesley [1963] find that vehicle speeds increased only 4–6 percent after the introduction of the Victoria Line in London. And this is on the dubious assumption that the speed increase induces no new vehicle traffic.) Because of this, the line's effect on the costs of using other modes is ignored. Also, since we're dealing for the moment with a situation of fixed residential and employment patterns, the characteristics of the users in each tract does not change with changes in the location of the line. Account is made for long run users at the end of the following section.

The [C_{2j} (line haul distance)] term gives the part of the time (and amenity) cost as well as the part of the fare that varies proportionately with line haul distance. Total fares are often computed in practice as a base fare plus a per mile charge. For example, Gannett Fleming et al. (1974) use 20¢ plus 6¢ per mile as the basis of fare computations and projected revenues for proposed extensions of the Lindenwold HSL. The base fare enters in the C_{0j} part of the formula cited above, while the per mile charge enters in the C_{2j} term. More complex fare schemes can also be handled by our optimal rail methodology after suitably revising the L_j formula (e.g., adding squared and higher order terms in line haul distance); however, we will limit ourselves here to the fairly straightforward linear fare case.

Line haul time is also assumed to vary linearly with distance, an assumption that is the same as saying average line haul speed between successive pickup points is constant. This is a fairly reasonable assumption, and any variations from it can again be accounted for by using a higher than first order polynomial in (line haul distance)—or by some other method. (The idea is that if the graph of line haul time on line haul distance is curvilinear, rather than linear, this graph may be approximated to an arbitrarily close degree by a polynomial function in line haul distance.) The optimal rail methodology that will be discussed below is a highly flexible tool, capable of withstanding these as well as many other changes of premise.

The C_{0j} term, in addition to picking up the parts of line haul time and money costs that are distance-invariant, also includes parking costs and walking and waiting times, all of which are assumed to be unaffected by the point of access to the rail line. While walking and waiting times can vary slightly from station to station (as when parking lot sizes vary and when there are express trains that skip some stations more than others), these variations are generally quite small. It does little injustice to take these costs as constant. (The assumption made here isn't even that strict since C_{0j} can vary with the origin tract. And further, the L_j total cost formula could be appropriately modified to allow these costs to vary with the point of access, generally without impairing the ability of our optimization methods to solve the required problem. It will be left to the reader's imagination to think of how he or she would modify the assumptions and then incorporate these changes into the optimal rail finding algorithms, discussed below.) Finally, since the rail line ends at the CBD, average egress costs are also part of the C_{0j} term.

Following the results of Chapter 3, the demand function we shall employ is the compressed logit (c logit). Of course, if c, the degree of compression, is set equal to 1, this becomes the ordinary logit. While we could derive optimal rail paths under linear or semilog (or other) demand functions, use of the c logit adds realism and puts the optimization algorithms to the task of dealing with a more complex demand form. The c logit can be written in the form:

$$p_j = q_j/q_j^* = c/[1 + \exp(-O_j + kC_{0j} + kC_{1j} \text{ [access distance]}$$
$$+ kC_{2j} \text{ [line haul distance]})] \quad (4.2)$$

where p_j = share of potential line users actually using the line, in the jth tract

q_j = number of line users in the jth tract

q_j^* = number of potential users in the jth tract

O_j = the sum of all regression coefficients times the value in the jth tract of the corresponding variables—except for variables representing line costs and their coefficients. In short, O_j, represents the effect on rail line demand and hence on line location of all the variables except line costs.

k = a (common) coefficient on total line cost

$\exp(\ )$ = the exponential function (base e).

Denoting the fares paid by those in the jth tract as t_j, total revenue for line use is:

$$R = \sum_{j=1}^{N} t_j p_j q_j^* \quad (4.3)$$

where N equals number of tracts. The fares, t_j, are again taken as varying linearly with line haul distance. This relation is discussed further for each access assumption in the following two sections.

All of the above discussion has been independent of which type of access path we assume line users to be taking. It is now time to make explicit our choice of access path assumptions.

THE REVENUE-MAXIMIZING RAIL LINE
UNDER VERTICAL ACCESS

The assumption employed in this section is about the simplest one which can be made without losing touch with reality. It is the vertical access path and is illustrated in Figure 4–1.

The rail line starts at the CBD, which is placed at the origin of the coordinate system, for convenience. The equation of the rail line is $y = f(x)$, and the terminal point of the line is at $(x_e, f(x_e))$. At $(x_b, f(x_b))$ is the closest suburban station to the CBD. Tract centroids are shown as dots in

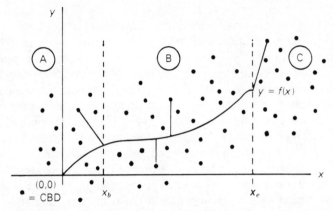

Figure 4–1. The Vertical Access Assumption.

the figure. It is assumed that the path of access to the line is determined for all users in a given tract by the location of the centroid of that tract (i.e., all users act as if they live at the centroid).

Now, we assume that all tracts with x coordinates greater than or equal to x_e (i.e., those tracts in region C) arrive at the rail line by straight line access to the final station at $(x_e, f(x_e))$. All those tracts with x coordinates less than or equal to x_b (i.e., tracts in region A) are assumed to employ straight line access to the first suburban station, at $(x_b, f(x_b))$. The remaining tracts, in region B, are assumed to gain access to the line by moving "vertically" (i.e., in the ordinate direction only) to the rail line.

While this seems to be a fairly reasonable access scheme, several comments are in order. The assumption of straight line access may at first seem a bit offensive, but in many cases it is a very close approximation of actual over the road distances. This is the case for the Lindenwold HSL (see, for example, Boyce and Allen [1972]). In cases where this assumption is not felt to be a close approximation, an average markup factor (of, say, 1.05 or 1.10 or 1.20) can be applied to straight line distances in order to bring them closer to an over the road distance figure. This markup factor can, of course, be allowed to vary from tract to tract.

The premise of vertical access for tracts in region B is a simple one, but it will be a fairly good assumption when the major roads passing through region B mostly run in a "vertical" direction. Of course, if most of the main roads run in one direction, but not the vertical one, the coordinate axes can merely be rotated, so that the assumption is satisfied!

The vertical access scheme also carries with it an assumption that will be employed throughout this book. It is that access to a finite number of explicit stations (aside from the first and last suburban stations), is not considered. Alternatively, we can say that the assumption is made that between x_b and x_e there is a high density of stations, such that the users have essentially universal access to the rail line. This is a simplification, but not too bad a one where, in fact, suburban stations are fairly close together.[3] In any case, consideration of the location and use of explicit stations (aside from the first and last) is outside the scope of this book. One may want to mark up access distance to the line for tracts in region B in order to reflect less than universal access. It is proposed that line haul distance be left unchanged—since the station may be closer or farther from the CBD than is supposed under the scheme here—with no real presumption existing in favor of either of these two possibilities. The markup factor for access distance can be included in the tract-specific C_{1j} factor and hence requires no change in the formal mathematics!

Recall from Chapter 1 that the optimal rail problem is to find the welfare-maximizing (here, for simplicity, the revenue-maximizing) line between the CBD—located at (0,0)—and some point in the suburbs. Not only must we find this point where the optimal line ends, but also the optimal path between the CBD and the endpoint.

The solution to the optimal rail problem proceeds in two parts. In the first part, we begin by choosing an arbitrary abscissa value, x_e, for the end of the rail line. Next, we solve by the methods discussed below for the optimal path, $y = f(x)$, running between the CBD and any point on the vertical line $x = x_e$. In the second part of the solution, we choose a new x_e value and solve again for the optimal line. And we continue—iterating over a grid or set of x_e values and finding the corresponding optimal line in each case. Then, finally, we choose the x_e value and corresponding rail path that give the greatest revenue.

To solve the revenue-maximizing problem for given x_e, we look at the costs of line use in the three types of tracts that have been distinguished (i.e., those in regions A, B, C). For type A tracts the cost of line use is:

$$L_j^A = C_{0j} + C_{1j} \sqrt{(x_j - x_b)^2 + (y_j - f(x_b))^2} + C_{2j} \int_0^{x_b} \sqrt{1 + (f'(x))^2}\, dx \quad (4.4)$$

where here, and throughout the chapter, we take the positive root whenever we take the square root of a quantity. Recall that (x_j, y_j) are the coordinates of the jth tract's centroid. Equation (4.4) makes use of the fact that the path length of $f(x)$ between $x = 0$ and $x = x_b$ is given by the indicated integral. Similarly, the costs of line use for type B and C tracts, respectively, are:

[3] Suburban stations do tend to be fairly close. For example, average spacing between the suburban stations of the Lindenwold HSL is about 1.6 miles. And there is a proposal for building an additional station between the Ashland and Haddonfield stops, where the gap is 3.2 miles.

$$L_j^B = C_{0j} + C_{1j}\left|y_j - f(x_j)\right| + C_{2j}\int_0^{x_j}\sqrt{1+(f'(x))^2}\,dx \tag{4.5}$$

$$L_j^C = C_{0j} + C_{1j}\sqrt{(x_j - x_e)^2 + (y_j - f(x_e))^2}$$
$$+ C_{2j}\int_0^{x_e}\sqrt{1+(f'(x))^2}\,dx \tag{4.6}$$

Note that $|z|$ stands for the absolute value of z.

Of all N tracts, we denote the number of type B tracts as N_b and the number of type A tracts as N_a. For later convenience we let the B tracts be the first group to be indexed. Accordingly, the centroids of the B tracts are (x_1,y_1), (x_2,y_2), . . . , (x_{N_b},y_{N_b}). Further, we index these so that $x_1 \leq x_2 \leq x_3 \leq, \ldots, \leq x_{N_b}$. We index the type A tracts next so that they are denoted: (x_{N_b+1},y_{N_b+1}), . . . , $(x_{N_b+N_a},y_{N_b+N_a})$. Finally, the type C tracts are indexed last, carrying subscripts from (N_b+N_a+1) to N.

As noted in the preceding section, fares are assumed to be linear in line haul distance. Hence we can write for all j:

$$t_j = r_1 + r_2 \text{ (line haul distance)} \tag{4.7}$$

Let revenue from type A, B, and C tracts be denoted as R^A, R^B, and R^C, respectively. Employing equations (4.2) through (4.7), we get total revenue as:

$$R = R^A + R^B + R^C \tag{4.8}$$

where

$$R^A = \sum_{j=N_b+1}^{N_b+N_a} [r_1 + r_2 \int_0^{x_b}\sqrt{1+(f'(x))^2}\,dx][cq_j^*]/[1 + \exp(-O_j + kC_{0j}$$
$$+ kC_{1j}\sqrt{(x_j - x_b)^2 + (y_j - f(x_b))^2} + kC_{2j}\int_0^{x_b}\sqrt{1+(f'(x))^2}\,dx)]$$

$$R^B = \sum_{j=1}^{N_b} [r_1 + r_2 \int_0^{x_j}\sqrt{1 + (f'(x))^2}\,dx][cq_j^*]/[1 + \exp(-O_j + kC_{0j}$$
$$+ kC_{1j}\left|y_j - f(x_j)\right| + kC_{2j}\int_0^{x_j}\sqrt{1+(f'(x))^2}\,dx)]$$

$$R^C = \sum_{j=N_b+N_a+1}^{N} [r_1 + r_2 \int_0^{x_e}\sqrt{1+(f'(x))^2}\,dx][cq_j^*]/[1 + \exp(-O_j + kC_{0j}$$
$$+ kC_{1j}\sqrt{(x_j - x_e)^2 + (y_j - f(x_e))^2} + kC_{2j}\int_0^{x_e}\sqrt{1+(f'(x))^2}\,dx)]$$

Choosing the path f such that R is maximized is the problem to be dealt with in this section. Note that everything else on the RHS of the above three subequations is assumed to be known—namely, $N, N_a, N_b, r_1, r_2, x_b,$ x_e, k, c—as well as $q_j^*, O_j, C_{0j}, C_{1j}, C_{2j}, x_j, y_j,$ for all j—are given.

How is this problem to be attacked? Perhaps a first thought is the two widely used optimal path-finding methods known as the calculus of variations and dynamic programming. As the reader can perhaps appreciate from the complexity of equation (4.8), use of the standard calculus of variations techniques is impossible. Dynamic programming, it also turns out, cannot be used to maximize equation (4.8), except under very restrictive conditions. Rather, we rely on two iterative techniques. The technique that will be employed in this section is known as the Euler finite difference method. In the following section, with least cost access, it will be more convenient to apply a different technique, known as the Ritz method. Both of these are called "direct methods" for solving the optimal path problem because their yield is the optimal path itself. This is in contrast to the calculus of variations, which is "indirect" because the yield is a differential equation that must then be solved for the optimizing path.

Let us turn now to the application of the Euler finite difference method to solving the maximization of equation (4.8). To use this method, we approximate f by a broken line segment (BLS) path. This is illustrated by Figure 4–2.

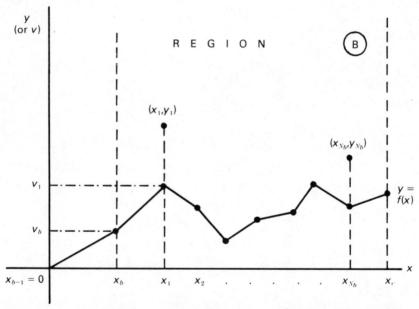

Figure 4–2. The BLS Path of the Euler Finite Difference Method.

A BLS is, of course, fully characterized by its vertexes, and so the problem of finding a maximizing path, f, is reduced to that of finding, in some sense, the maximizing set of vertex points. What we do here is to take as given the abscissa (x) values of the set of vertex points and solve for each of their ordinate (v) values. The actual choice of the set of abscissa values is arbitrary—within the limits of having a fine enough grid so that the results are useful for planning purposes. In order to keep the notation as simple as possible, we have taken the set of given abscissa values of the vertexes of the line as coinciding with x_b and x_e and with the abscissa values of the type B tracts—that is, as the set $[x_b, x_1, \ldots, x_{N_b}, x_e]$. The optimal rail problem is reduced to that of finding the corresponding set of ordinate values, $[v_b, v_1, \ldots, v_{N_b}, v_e]$, such that revenue is maximized.

With only a complication in notation and slight changes in formula, we can, of course, take a finer or a coarser grid than that which is used here. Also, we need not assume that grid points will coincide with the abscissa values of type B tracts; this is only for simplicity of representation, not ease of computation. We point out that by making the grid of x values fine enough, the resulting BLS path can be made as close as is desired to any arbitrary, smooth f.

With a BLS path, path length, previously found by integration, can now be represented as a simple sum. For example, the line haul distance from the end of the line at (x_e, v_e) to the CBD is now:

$$\sum_{j=b}^{e} \sqrt{(x_j - x_{j-1})^2 + (v_j - v_{j-1})^2} \tag{4.9}$$

Note that for convenience of representation we have taken the CBD $= (0,0) = (x_{b-1}, v_{b-1})$; and in the indexes we count up by units from $b-1$ to b to 1 to 2 to $\ldots$ to N_b to e. Access distance from the jth tract for $1 \leqslant j \leqslant N_b$ to the line is simply $|y_j - v_j|$; for other j, access distance is the straight line distance to the first or last stations—as before. Within the class of BLS paths, we can rewrite equation (4.8), total revenue, as:

$$R = R^A + R^B + R^C \tag{4.10}$$

where

$$R^A = \sum_{j=N_b+1}^{N_b+N_a} [r_1 + r_2\sqrt{x_b^2 + v_b^2}][cq_j^*]/[1 + \exp(-O_j + kC_{0j}$$

$$+ kC_{1j}\sqrt{(x_j - x_b)^2 + (y_j - v_b)^2} + kC_{2j}\sqrt{x_b^2 + v_b^2})]$$

$$R^B = \sum_{j=1}^{N_b} [r_1 + r_2 \sum_{k=b}^{j} \sqrt{(x_k-x_{k-1})^2 + (v_k-v_{k-1})^2}] [cq_j^*]/[1 + \exp(-O_j$$

$$+ kC_{0j} + kC_{1j} |y_j-v_j| + kC_{2j} \sum_{k=b}^{j} \sqrt{(x_k-x_{k-1})^2 + (v_k-v_{k-1})^2})]$$

$$R^C = \sum_{j=N_b+N_a+1}^{N} [r_1 + r_2 \sum_{k=b}^{e} \sqrt{(x_k-x_{k-1})^2+(v_k-v_{k-1})^2}] [cq_j^*]/[1 + \exp(-O_j + kC_{0j}$$

$$+ kC_{1j} \sqrt{(x_j-x_e)^2 + (y_j-v_e)^2} + kC_{2j} \sum_{k=b}^{e} \sqrt{(x_k-x_{k-1})^2+(v_k-v_{k-1})^2})]$$

Note that everything in equation (4.10) is known except the (N_b+2) variables: $v_b, v_1, v_2, \ldots, v_{N_b}, v_e$. To find the value of these variables such that R is maximized is a simple matter. We may use numerical "hill climbing" methods, which do or do not rely on taking the partial derivatives of (4.10). If one chooses to use a method that employs partial derivatives, it should be noted that all of the above terms are everywhere differentiable in all the vs—except for the access distance expressions when access distance equals 0 (i.e., when a line vertex coincides with a tract centroid). In the unlikely event that in the course of iterating to solution we hit upon such a case—say for the kth tract—then $\dfrac{\partial R}{\partial v_k}$ will fail to exist. There are many simple ways out of this minor problem. One is to shift or perturb the centroid ordinate value, y_k, slightly by adding a minute random number to it. This leaves the classification of the tract (type A, B, or C) and the access point unchanged, but ensures that the required derivative will exist. Since the calculation of centroid measures such as y_k is subject to some error anyway, we do not affect matters substantively by doing this. We will come upon other cases where perturbation will prove an easy and useful method for dealing with expressions that exist almost everywhere (i.e., everywhere except on a set of measure 0).

Choice of numerical maximization algorithms depends on many factors, not the least of which is which routines are readily available in progammed form. This matter will not be dealt with further here, except to note that one possibility for solution is to find the first partial derivatives of R and to set each of these equal to 0. This will result in N_b+2 nonlinear equations in as many unknowns, which may then be solved iteratively by expanding each in a linear (first order) Taylor series around the previous "guess" and solving the linear equations for a new set of values. Since there is no guarantee of there being a single critical point, one would want to try different initial guesses in order to try and be sure that she or he has found a global maximum.

The alert reader may have noticed that the revenue maximization problem we have solved is a static one, when in fact we must consider maximization of a discounted stream of revenues over time. That is, the revenue expression in equation (4.10) is revenue for one time period. If, however, the independent variables and parameters of the demand function $(c, k, O_j, C_{0j}, C_{1j}, C_{2j}, q_j^*$—for all $j)$, as well as the fare parameters (r_1, r_2), do not change over time, then the R expression in equation (4.10) holds for all periods. In such a case, the present value of all future revenues, assuming a discount rate of i and an operating life of h years, is $= R \sum_{t=1}^{h} 1/(1+i)^t$. Since this is proportional to R, maximization of R (revenue in one year) will imply maximization of the present value of the full revenue stream.

If, on the other hand, the independent variables and parameters of the demand function or the fare parameters change over time (we do, in fact, expect some of this) then we will have a series of revenue terms, $R^{(t)}$, one for each year of operation of the line. The difference between the $R^{(t)}$ terms will not, of course, be in the crucial v variables, but rather in parameters like $O_j^{(t)}$ and $q_j^{*(t)}$. (The (t) superscript is appended to indicate that the parameter may change from period to period.) To find the rail line that maximizes the present value of all revenues we merely substitute a time-varying version of equation (4.10) into the expression:

$$PV_r = \sum_{t=1}^{h} R^{(t)}/(1+i)^t \tag{4.11}$$

and maximize PV_r with respect to each of the vs. This is a straightforward extension of maximizing equation (4.10), and needs no further comment.

Another wrinkle that has been finessed in the preceeding discussion is the fact that we have omitted nonwork trip demand—and hence nonwork revenue—from equations (4.10) and (4.11). In addition, certain types of work trips may also have been omitted (e.g., reverse haul, long run). If, as is quite possible, we model total revenue as a simple markup on the work trip revenue captured in equation (4.10), then what we have already done (maximization of R or PV_r) is sufficient. If, on the other hand, we have one or more additional and separate demand relations for the omitted trip types, then we need to find the corresponding revenue expressions (along the lines of R or PV_r) and maximize the total revenue for all trip types over the choice of all BLS rail lines. Again, we use the rail line's effect on access and line haul costs as the crucial nexus between line location and revenue. As pointed out in Chapter 3, we must have closed form demand relations for all trip types. It should now be clear why this is necessary. An abstract mode type relation, giving predicted line ridership as a function of line costs (hence of line haul and access distance), is well suited to the purposes here.

THE REVENUE-MAXIMIZING RAIL LINE
UNDER LEAST TOTAL COST ACCESS

If the road system does not have the unidirectional dominancy required to make vertical access a reasonable assumption, it may have characteristics more suited to least total cost access. Under least total cost (LTC), we assume that the rail-using commuter gains access to the line at a point where total journey costs are minimized. This is a very appealing behavioral assumption. It is subject to the rather trivial physical limitation that there be sufficient density in the road network so that as a practical matter access to points all along the rail line is possible. In the Lindenwold HSL, roads cross the line every few hundred feet—close enough in a journey of several miles! In addition, we might require that suburban stations be fairly close together; however, using tract-specific markup factors on total cost takes away much of the need for this closeness assumption. This is similar in principle to using the markup on access distance for type B tracts, discussed in the previous section.

We shall assume that access distance from each tract centroid to all points on the line is the straight line distance (or a markup of this distance—the markup factor being the same regardless of the line access point) and that access speed varies only with the tract (not the access point). We needn't make these assumptions. We could undertake to gather the information necessary to estimate an over the road distance gradient and an over the road speed gradient—for each tract—showing the actual distance and speed from each census tract centroid to all other points in the area of interest. The calculations of this section do not allow for such gradients, since it is felt that they will probably not be used in practice. The simpler assumptions are probably close enough for most purposes, in all likelihood being well within the error bounds of statistical estimation and quite small compared with prediction errors. The presence of these gradients would therefore only encumber the mathematical exposition.

The mathematics of LTC access can best be shown with the aid of Figure 4–3. Let the rail line be denoted $y = f(x)$, as usual. Consider users at the point (x_j, y_j), the jth tract centroid, making the decision on where to access the line. Let z_j be the (as yet unknown) abscissa value of the access point. As before, let total journey costs be represented as $L_j = C_{0j} + C_{1j}$ (access distance) $+ C_{2j}$ (line haul distance), where, again, access distance

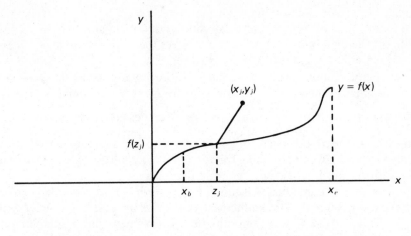

Figure 4–3. The Least Total Cost Access Assumption.

is straight line distance. As before, a markup on this can be incorporated in the C_{1j} factor. Total journey costs can be rewritten as:

$$L_j = C_{0j} + C_{1j} \sqrt{(x_j-z_j)^2 + (y_j-f(z_j))^2} + C_{2j} \int_0^{z_j} \sqrt{1+(f'(x))^2}\, dx \qquad (4.12)$$

If the minimizing z_j falls somewhere within the admissible range of abscissa values, $[x_b, x_e]$ (i.e., between the first and last stations), then we can minimize L_j by simple calculus. That is, we merely set $\dfrac{\partial L_j}{\partial z_j} = 0$ and solve for z_j. Applying the fundamental theorem of integral calculus in order to differentiate the integral in equation (4.12), we get:

$$\frac{\partial L_j}{\partial z_j} = -C_{1j} \left[(x_j-z_j)+(y_j-f(z_j))f'(z_j) \right] / \sqrt{(x_j-z_j)^2 + (y_j-f(z_j))^2}$$

$$+ C_{2j} \sqrt{1+(f'(z_j))^2} = 0 \quad (4.13)$$

Now we can use any of a number of iterative techniques (e.g., Newton-Raphson) to solve for z_j in (4.13). If there is more than one admissible root, we need only calculate the values of cost (L_j) corresponding to each root and to select the one that gives minimum total cost. In addition, we must check the endpoints of the interval (x_b and x_e) to see whether the minimum total cost access point is at one of these two points. In addition to checking for a corner minimum, evaluating total cost at the endpoints provides the necessary check that an interior critical point is indeed a minimum (not a maximum or saddle point). If L_j is greater at the endpoints than at an alleged interior minimum, then the alleged minimum is indeed a minimum. If L_j is smaller at one of the endpoints than at an alleged interior minimum, then the commuter's point of access will be that endpoint. In short, we find all admissible roots of equation (4.13), add to this set the endpoints (x_b and x_e), and select the abscissa value of access that minimizes L_j—out of these possibilities.

A minor technical matter should also be noted. As in the previous section, in the unlikely event that during the course of obtaining solutions, access distance = $\sqrt{(x_j-z_j)^2 + (y_j-f(z_j))^2}$ becomes zero, then $\dfrac{\partial L_j}{\partial z_j}$ will fail to exist. Again, the best way out seems to be to add a minute perturbation to the centroid of the offending tract, so that the centroid is moved off the path of the rail line and the required derivative exists.

Note that in equations (4.12) and (4.13) we have used the derivative, $f'(x)$, of the rail path. Unlike the case of vertical access, it is simpler with LTC access to deal with smooth (i.e., everywhere differentiable) rail paths than with BLS paths (where the derivative of $y=f(x)$ fails to exist at every vertex point). The reason for this will be seen more clearly in the next chapter, where finding the optimal line under LTC access and under certain types of constraints necessitates a return to using a BLS path (or a generalization of a BLS). It will be seen there that for every kink in the rail line, an additional solution of an equation like (4.13) must be performed.

Because of the computational advantage of using a smooth rail path, we employ here the Ritz optimal path-finding method, rather than the Euler finite difference method employed in the previous section. All that is really required for the Ritz method is that we postulate a functional form for $f(x)$, say polynomial (through the origin). That is, approximate any arbitrary $f(x)$ by the expression: $y = a_1x + a_2x^2 + \ldots + a_nx^n$. The problem of finding an optimal path is then reduced, as with the Euler method, to the multivariable calculus problem of finding optimal values of a finite set of unknown parameters, here $[a_1,a_2, \ldots , a_n]$. Of course, an ordinary polynomial need not be used. Another candidate is a function composed of a limited number of terms from a discrete Fourier series. We would probably want to set the minimum period of the sine and cosine functions to a length greater than the likely length of the line, in order to avoid the probably undesirable periodic characteristics of these trigonometric relations. Further, almost any other functional form, f, with unknown parameters, which allows the rail path to take on a wide variety of shapes, is acceptable. The only conditions that must be met are that f' and f'' exist, and that the partial derivatives of f and f' with respect to all the parameters of f exist and be continuous, and that we be able to evaluate line haul distance = $\displaystyle\int_0^{z_j}\sqrt{1+(f'(x))^2}\, dx$ as a closed form function.

This last integrability condition must be met in order to be able to evaluate L_j in equation (4.12). This is necessary in order to be able to compare corner and interior solutions. Uncountably many functions exist that satisfy all these conditions!

Gelfand and Fomin (1963: 196f) point out that in many applications of the Ritz method, a satisfactory approximation to the exact f solution is obtained using only a small number of additive terms. Of course, the more terms that are added to the functional form, the closer one can come to the exact solution. This is proved under broad regularity conditions for the Ritz method, as well as for the Euler method (with respect to the number of vertexes—rather than the number of terms in the function), by Gelfand and Fomin (1963: ch. 8). This is an important result and is the basis of the previous claim that the direct method approximation can be pushed arbitrarily close to the true solution.

Having discussed how to find the least total cost access point for any given rail line $y = f(x)$, and having discussed the criteria for choosing a class of fs to work with, we now turn to the question of revenue maximization. As in the preceding section, it will be convenient to deal with a static revenue expression that encompasses only the usual class of work trips. The extension to finding the line that maximizes the present value of all revenues from all types of trips on the line is straightforward and has already been discussed at the end of the prior section. No new substantive considerations enter with the change from the Euler to the Ritz method.

As in the previous section, we employ a c logit demand function. For any given f and set of z_j access points, line use costs are given by equation (4.12), above. Ridership for the jth tract is, therefore:

$$p_j = q_j/q^* = c/[1 + \exp(-O_j + kC_{0j} + kC_{1j} \sqrt{(x_j - z_j)^2 + (y_j - f(z_j))^2}$$

$$+ kC_{2j} \int_0^{z_j} \sqrt{1 + (f'(x))^2} \, dx)] \quad (4.14)$$

And under the usual assumption, that fares (t_j) rise linearly with line haul distance, we have that:

$$t_j = r_1 + r_2 \int_0^{z_j} \sqrt{1 + (f'(x))^2} \, dx \quad (4.15)$$

Finally, total revenue is:

$$R = \sum_{j=1}^{N} [r_1 + r_2 \int_0^{z_j} \sqrt{1 + (f'(x))^2} \, dx] \, [cq_j^*]/$$

$$[1 + \exp(-O_j + kC_{0j} + kC_{1j} \sqrt{(x_j - z_j)^2 + (y_j - f(z_j))^2}$$

$$+ kC_{2j} \int_0^{z_j} \sqrt{1 + (f'(x))^2} \, dx)] \quad (4.16)$$

Recall that we have assumed that the indicated integrals can be expressed in closed form. As such, we can rewrite the above integrals as $[F(z_j)-F(0)]$ where $F'(x) = \sqrt{1+(f'(x))^2}$. This substitution can also be made in equation (4.12), where we will need an explicit representation in order to compute total costs and check for an endpoint and overall minimum solution.

The optimal rail problem addressed in this section is to find the value of the set of parameters that underlie f such that revenue is maximized, subject to the condition that least total cost access is used. As in the previous section, we do this for rail lines running between the origin (CBD) and the vertical line $x = x_e$. As mentioned in that section, we can then search over a grid of x_e values in order to find the *optimum optimorum* rail line.

The solution to this problem is straightforward, given the framework that we have set up. For any given set of access points, $[z_j, j = 1, \ldots, N]$ and known values of parameters appearing in equation (4.16) (namely N, r_1, r_2, k, c, as well as $q_j^*, O_j, C_{0j}, C_{1j}, C_{2j}, x_j, y_j$—for all j), we see that R is a function only of the parameters underlying f. Let the vector of these parameters be denoted $\underline{P}$. To find the revenue maximizing rail line, we start by calculating $\dfrac{\partial R}{\partial \underline{P}}$ in equation (4.16), and then we set each of these derivative expressions equal to zero. (The somewhat unusual nature of the required derivative is discussed below.) This gives the set of conditions for maximization of revenue (one equation for each unknown parameter). Solving these simultaneously with N equations like (4.13) (one for each tract), which yield the set of LTC z_js, yields simultaneously the revenue-maximizing rail line and the least cost access points for each tract. Let us examine this procedure more closely.

Assume there are m entries in the vector $\underline{P}$. From equation (4.16), denote $\dfrac{\partial R}{\partial P_i}$ as R_i, for simplicity. Note that R_i will depend on $\underline{P}$ as well as on $[z_1, \ldots, z_N]$. In equation (4.13), denote $\dfrac{\partial L_j}{\partial z_j}$ as g_j, for simplicity. Note that g_j depends on $\underline{P}$ and z_j. We can write our simultaneous system of $(N+m)$ optimization equations in $(N+m)$ unknowns as:

$$
\left|
\begin{array}{l}
R_1 (P_1, \ldots, P_m, z_1, \ldots, z_N) = 0 \\
.\quad . \qquad\quad .\quad . \qquad\quad .\quad .\ . \\
.\quad . \qquad\quad .\quad . \qquad\quad .\quad .\ . \\
R_m(P_1, \ldots, P_m, z_1, \ldots, z_N) = 0
\end{array}
\right.
\qquad (4.17)
$$

$$
\begin{bmatrix}
g_1 (P_1, \ldots, P_m, z_1) = 0 \\
\cdot \quad \cdot \qquad\qquad \cdot \quad \cdot \quad \cdot \quad \cdot \\
\cdot \quad \cdot \qquad\qquad \cdot \quad \cdot \quad \cdot \quad \cdot \\
\cdot \quad \cdot \qquad\qquad \cdot \quad \cdot \quad \cdot \quad \cdot \\
g_N(P_1, \ldots, P_m, z_N) = 0
\end{bmatrix}
\tag{4.18}
$$

Now, recall from the discussion above that equations like those in (4.18) are alone not enough to characterize LTC access. This solution may yield inadmissible abscissa values (i.e., values lying outside of the $[x_b, x_e]$ interval) or nonminimums. In short, total cost (L_j) at the endpoints must be computed and checked against the total cost associated with all admissible values gotten from solving $g_j = 0$. This must be done at every iteration.

One easy way of solving equations (4.17) and (4.18) simultaneously is to use a Taylor series block improvement method (see, for example, Arden and Astill [1970: 146f]). The following is one possibility: (1) Guess initial values of $[P_1, \ldots, P_m]$. (2) Given these parameters for the optimal rail line, solve each of the g_j equations in (4.18) for its single unknown z_j. Do this perhaps by the Newton-Raphson (linear Taylor series) method (see Arden and Astill [1970: 54ff]). For each g_j in turn check all these roots for admissibility and check also whether an endpoint solution will give a lower value of total cost. (3) Having derived a set of access points, $[z_1, \ldots, z_N]$, in this way, use these values to get a new guess on $\underline{P}$—from equation (4.17). One method for doing this is to expand each of the equations in (4.17) in a linear Taylor series about the initial guess on $\underline{P}$, given the derived values of $[z_1, \ldots, z_N]$. Solve these linearized equations for new values of $\underline{P}$. Repeat steps (2) and (3) until convergence (i.e., until successive values of the variables differ by less than a preselected small amount). We shall not dwell here on the fine points of such numerical procedures, other than to say that with a reasonable initial guess, they should yield the desired solution. The interested reader is referred to numerical methods texts, such as Arden and Astill (1970), for more information on the convergence and other properties of various solution algorithms.

It should be remarked that the basic form of each of the R_j derivatives (not just the value of R_j—but also which terms are included in the expression) is affected by whether there are any endpoint solutions for the $[z_1, \ldots, z_N]$. It turns out that a term will be dropped in each of these derivatives for every z_j that is a true corner solution. The truth of this will emerge as we look more closely at the R_j derivatives.

The first, and rather confusing sounding, fact to be noticed is that each of the derivatives $R_j = \dfrac{\partial R}{\partial P_j}$ is really what may more correctly be called a total partial derivative. To see what this means let us rewrite equation (4.16), substituting $[F(z_j,\underline{P}) - F(0,\underline{P})]$ for $\int_0^{z_j} \sqrt{1+(f'(x))^2}\, dx$. That is:

$$R = \sum_{j=1}^{N} [r_1 + r_2[F(z_j,\underline{P})-F(0,\underline{P})]]\, [cq_j^*]/$$

$$[1 + \exp(-O_j+kC_{0j}+kC_{1j}\sqrt{(x_j-z_j)^2+(y_j-f(z_j))^2}$$

$$+ kC_{2j}[F(z_j,\underline{P}) - F(0,\underline{P})])] \tag{4.19}$$

Now, in calculating the change in R for a small change in P_j (say), we might be tempted to limit our differentiation to the $F(z_j,\underline{P})$ and $F(0,\underline{P})$ terms—wherein P_j appears explicitly. That is, we might consider taking the partial derivative $\dfrac{\partial R}{\partial P_j}$ for given $[z_1,\ldots,z_N]$, as well as given $[P_1,\ldots,P_{j-1},P_{j+1},\ldots,P_m]$. However, this would represent only part of the story. It must also be recognized that when P_j changes slightly, the rail line is moved slightly and all of the least total cost access points—hence all of the $z_{(.)}$s—may also change a little.[4] Therefore, in computing the effect on revenue of a change in P_j (holding all other variables in $\underline{P}$ constant), we must employ the following total partial derivative, which we redenote $R_j = \dfrac{dR}{\partial P_j}$:

$$\frac{dR}{\partial P_j} = \frac{\partial R}{\partial P_j} + \frac{\partial R}{\partial z_1}\frac{\partial z_1}{\partial P_j} + \ldots + \frac{\partial R}{\partial z_N}\frac{\partial z_N}{\partial P_j} \tag{4.20}$$

This gives the total change in revenue, allowing P_j as well as $[z_1,\ldots,z_N]$ to vary. This is surely the R_j concept that we want to use in equation (4.17).

Now the $\dfrac{\partial R}{\partial P_j}$ and $\dfrac{\partial R}{\partial z_1},\ldots,\dfrac{\partial R}{\partial z_N}$ expressions can be gotten directly from doing the indicated differentiation on equation (4.19). But how are we to get $\dfrac{\partial z_1}{\partial P_j},\ldots,\dfrac{\partial z_N}{\partial P_j}$, the variation in access point abscissa values for a change in P_j? The answer is that we use equation (4.13), where each $z_{(.)}$ is defined implicitly as a function of the $\underline{P}$. Rewriting equation (4.13) to show the role of $\underline{P}$, and considering the cost minimizing condition for the ith access point, we have:

---

[4] Thanks to Professor Stephen Ross for clarifying this point.

$$-C_{1i}[(x_i-z_i)+(y_i-f(z_i,\underline{P}))f'(z_i,\underline{P})]/\sqrt{(x_i-z_i)^2 + (y_i -f(z_i,\underline{P}))^2}$$

$$+ C_{2i} \sqrt{1 + (f'(z_i,P))^2} = 0 \quad (4.21)$$

where $f'(z_i,P)$ should be interpreted as $\dfrac{\partial f(z_i,P)}{\partial z_i}$. Equation (4.21) is of the general implicit form $h(z_i,P_1, \ldots , P_m) = 0$. Now, to obtain the variation in z_i for an infinitesimal change in P_j, we use the implicit function rule. This says that $\dfrac{\partial z_i}{\partial P_j} = - \dfrac{\partial h}{\partial P_j} \bigg/ \dfrac{\partial h}{\partial z_i}$. It is a simple matter to perform the indicated partial differentiation on h, h being differentiable under our assumption that f and f' are differentiable. Also note that since we are finding $\dfrac{\partial h}{\partial z_i} = \dfrac{\partial^2 L_i}{\partial z_i^2}$ at a minimum point (not a point of inflection— where the second derivative of L_i is 0), we are guaranteed that, locally, $\dfrac{\partial h}{\partial z_i} \neq 0$. This is the condition that must be met in order to apply the implicit function rule.

All of this discussion on how to find $\dfrac{\partial z_i}{\partial P_j}$ using the implicit function rule is fine so long as z_i is an analytic, rather than a cornerpoint, minimum. Only then will equation (4.21) hold. The entire discussion may be short circuited if the LTC access point is at an endpoint (that is, at the first or last station) and if the endpoint coordinates do not satisfy equation (4.21)—that is, we have a true corner, rather than an analytic, solution. If z_i is such a corner solution, changing any of the rail line parameters, $\underline{P}$, infinitesimally will not affect z_i at all. The users in the ith tract will still gain access to the line at the same endpoint. In this case, $\dfrac{\partial z_i}{\partial P} = 0$, and so one term drops out of each of the $\dfrac{\partial R}{\partial P_j} = 0$ expressions, as noted above.[5]

---

[5] Note that in the unlikely event that we happen to get an endpoint minimum as a calculus solution for z_i (i.e., the coordinates of the endpoint satisfy equation (4.21) and result in the minimum total cost of all admissible access points), then $\partial z_i/\partial P_j$ may well be ambiguous for all j. Suppose the commuters of the ith tract gain access to the line at $z_i=x_b$. An infinitesimal increase in P_j may, for example, make these commuters want to access the line closer to the origin and, hence, reinforce their use of the first station. On the other hand, an infinitesimal decrease in P_j may push the x access value higher. In short, the right hand partial of $\partial z_i/\partial P_j$ may be 0 while the left hand partial may be negative—leading to an indeterminate value for $\partial z_i/\partial P_j$.

Another highly unlikely situation in which $\partial z_i/\partial P_j$ is indeterminate is when there are two (or more) admissible values of z_i that yield identical and minimizing values of total cost. In this case, altering the rail line by changing P_j infinitesimally will most likely result in two (or more) different values for $\partial z_i/\partial P_j$.

An Example

We now do a simple example to illustrate finding the least cost access points and the revenue-maximizing rail line. The example chosen is that of a linear rail line, $y=bx$. Note that b takes the place of $\underline{P}$ in the above equations. The object is to find the revenue-maximizing b under LTC access. First we look at the cost minimization part.

For the jth tract, access distance is $\sqrt{(x_j-z_j)^2 + (y_j-bz_j)^2}$, and line haul distance is $\sqrt{z_j^2+(bz_j)^2} = z_j\sqrt{1+b^2}$. Accordingly, total cost is:

$$L_j = C_{0j} + C_{1j}\sqrt{(x_j-z_j)^2+(y_j-bz_j)^2} + C_{2j}z_j\sqrt{1+b^2} \qquad (4.22)$$

Taking the partial of L_j with respect to z_j, we get the following equation for a noncorner minimum:

$$-C_{1j}[(x_j-z_j)+b(y_j-bz_j)]/\sqrt{(x_j-z_j)^2 + (y_j-bz_j)^2}+C_{2j}\sqrt{1+b^2} = 0 \qquad (4.23)$$

Putting the $C_{2j}\sqrt{1+b^2}$ term on the right hand side of the equation, multiplying both sides by $\sqrt{(x_j-z_j)^2+(y_j-bz_j)^2}$, squaring both sides, and collecting terms, we get the following second degree polynomial in z_j:

$$[(C_{2j}^2-C_{1j}^2)(1+b^2)^2]z_j^2 - 2[(C_{2j}^2-C_{1j}^2)(1+b^2)$$
$$(x_j+by_j)]z_j + [(C_{2j}^2-C_{1j}^2)(x_j^2+b^2y_j^2) +$$
$$(C_{2j}^2y_j^2 + C_{2j}^2b^2x_j^2 - 2C_{1j}^2bx_jy_j)] = 0 \qquad (4.24)$$

Solving for z_j, we get, after some cancelling of terms, the following two solutions:

$$z_j = \frac{x_j+by_j}{1+b^2} \pm \sqrt{(C_{1j}^2-C_{2j}^2)(C_{2j}^2(y_j+bx_j)^2 - C_{1j}^2(4bx_jy_j))}$$

$$/[-(C_{1j}^2-C_{2j}^2)(1+b^2)] \qquad (4.25)$$

Now which root, the positive or the negative, are we to take? While normally the question would be answered by numerically finding both roots and comparing their associated L_j values (total costs), a bit of deduction suffices in this simple example. Referring to Figure 4–4, the rail line is represented by the solid line with equation $y=bx$. Also shown is the perpendicular from the centroid of tract j at (x_j,y_j) to the rail line. Since

---

Both of these situations have essentially 0 percent chance of occurring. However, should they crop up, all one need do to eliminate the ambiguity in $\partial z_i/\partial P_i$ is to perturb the coordinates of the ith tract's centroid slightly and recalculate the minimizing value(s) of z_i. The ambiguity should then disappear.

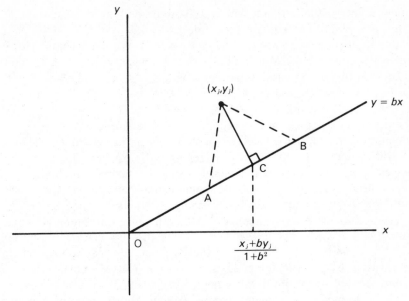

Figure 4-4. Two Access Paths to the Linear Rail Line.

the slope of this perpendicular is $-1/b$ and goes through (x_j, y_j), the equation of this normal line is $(y-y_j)=-(1/b)(x-x_j)$ or $y = -x/b + y_j + x_j/b$. The intersection of the perpendicular with the rail line occurs, therefore, at $bx = -x/b + y_j + x_j/b$, or at $x = (x_j+by_j)/(1+b^2)$. This is exactly the first term in equation (4.25). Assuming the two roots in equation (4.25) are real (and unequal), we can see clearly that they must call for access to a pair of points like A and B, equally distant along the x axis from C. (If the roots are real and equal, there's no ambiguity, of course, and access is at C.) Clearly, LTC access calls for using A; hence, we choose the root in equation (4.25), which results in the entire second term of that equation being negative. The other (nonminimum) critical point, at B, is a point of inflection; it cannot be a maximum, since total costs can be increased indefinitely by reaching the line at points successively farther out on the OA ray.

While A is indicated by our analysis as the minimum cost access point,[6] it may not be an admissible solution. That is, the abscissa value of A may be less than x_b or greater than x_e. In this case, the endpoint closest to A will turn out to be the LTC access point. (Why?) Also, if the solution to equation (4.25) results in a pair of imaginary roots, then the LTC access point will be one of the two endpoints—since there are no (real-valued)

---

[6] Checking the second order conditions verifies this.

critical points within the interval $[x_b, x_e]$—and so L_j must be monotonic within this range (indeed, on the whole real line).

Note that whenever $C_{1j} < C_{2j}$, we get a pair of imaginary roots. This is because in equation (4.25) the square root of a negative number is taken. To see that this is so merely note that when $C_{1j} < C_{2j}$: $(C_{1j}^2 - C_{2j}^2) < 0$, and since $(y_j + bx_j)^2 \geqslant 4bx_jy_j$ always (since $(y_j - bx_j)^2 \geqslant 0$), then $C_{2j}^2(y_j + bx_j)^2 - C_{1j}^2(4bx_jy_j) > 0$, assuming $(x_j, y_j) \neq (0,0)$. This is intuitively obvious: If per mile access costs (C_{1j}) are less than per mile line haul costs (C_{2j}), then a cost-minimizing commuter will not go out of her or his way to use the line, but will rather try to go all the way to the CBD by car—this being the shortest in distance as well as being the per mile cheapest method. A rail user in these circumstances will use the first suburban station. There is no necessary contradiction in actually being a rail user, since she or he avoids the downtown parking costs, which a full auto commuter pays. Note, by the way, that if the roots of equation (4.25) are real, then $(C_{1j}^2 - C_{2j}^2)$ must be nonnegative, and the LTC solution will involve taking the positive (+) part of the ambiguous ($\pm$) sign. This will ensure that the second term of equation (4.25) is negative, as called for above. [7]

Having looked at LTC access, let us examine the revenue-maximizing choice of b. Using equation (4.16) or equation (4.19) above, total revenue is:

$$R = \sum_{j=1}^{N} [r_1 + r_2 z_j \sqrt{1+b^2}][cq_j^*]/[1+\exp(\ )], \tag{4.26}$$

where we let

$$\exp(\ ) = \exp(-O_j + kC_{0j} + kC_{1j}\sqrt{(x_j - z_j)^2 + (y_j - bz_j)^2} + kC_{2j}z_j\sqrt{1+b^2}) \tag{4.27}$$

Recall that from the above discussion, we must find the partial derivative of R with respect to b and set this equal to 0. Further, since the choice of b may affect the choice of z_js, what we really want to set equal to 0 is the total partial of R with respect to b. While the partial $\dfrac{\partial R}{\partial b}$ plays a role in the total partial, $\dfrac{dR}{\partial b}$, it is not the full story. Since equations (4.26) and (4.27) are differentiable, we can find, using the simple product rule for differentiation:

---

[7] On the other hand, we must take the negative (−) part in order to get the second term of equation (4.25) positive if the rail line is in the second and third, rather than the usual first and fourth quadrants.

$$\frac{\partial R}{\partial b} = \sum_{j=1}^{N} [r_1 + r_2 z_j b/\sqrt{1+b^2}][cq_j^*] / [1+\exp(\ )]$$

$$+ [r_1 + r_2 z_j \sqrt{1+b^2}][cq_j^*][-\exp(\ )][kC_{2j}z_j b/\sqrt{1+b^2}$$

$$- kC_{1j}z_j(y_j - bz_j) / \sqrt{(x_j - z_j)^2 + (y_j - bz_j)^2}]$$

$$/ [1+\exp(\ )]^2 \qquad (4.28)$$

In addition, we need for all j the $\dfrac{\partial R}{\partial z_j}$ and $\dfrac{\partial z_j}{\partial b}$ partials. The first of these is readily derived from equations (4.26) and (4.27):

$$\frac{\partial R}{\partial z_j} = [r_1 + r_2\sqrt{1+b^2}][cq_j^*]/[1+\exp(\ )] + [r_1 + r_2 z_j\sqrt{1+b^2}]$$

$$[cq_j^*][-\exp(\ )][kC_{2j}\sqrt{1+b^2} - kC_{1j}[(x_j - z_j) + b(y_j - bz_j)]$$

$$/\sqrt{(x_j - z_j)^2 + (y_j - bz_j)^2}]/[1+\exp(\ )]^2 \qquad (4.29)$$

The second of these, $\dfrac{\partial z_j}{\partial b}$, is derived from equation (4.25)—so long as z_j is a noncorner point minimum. Note that we needn't fall back on the implicit function rule in the case at hand, since we have an explicit expression for real z_j.

$$\frac{\partial z_j}{\partial b} = [y_j(1+b^2) - 2b(x_j + by_j)]/[1+b^2]^2 - (1/2)[((C_{1j}^2 - C_{2j}^2)$$

$$(2C_{2j}^2 x_j(y_j + bx_j) - 4C_{1j}^2 x_j y_j]/\sqrt{(C_{1j}^2 - C_{2j}^2)(C_{2j}^2(y_j + bx_j)^2 - C_{1j}^2(4bx_j y_j))}$$

$$[(C_{1j}^2 - C_{2j}^2)(1+b^2)] + \sqrt{(C_{1j}^2 - C_{2j}^2)(C_{2j}^2(y_j + bx_j)^2 - C_{1j}^2(4bx_j y_j))}$$

$$[2b/(C_{1j}^2 - C_{2j}^2)(1+b^2)^2] \qquad (4.30)$$

Now we can use equation (4.20) in conjunction with equations (4.27) through (4.30) to derive the total partial $\dfrac{dR}{\partial b}$. Setting this total partial equal to 0 and solving it simultaneously with the positive root of equation (4.25) for all $j = 1, \ldots, N$ (least cost access conditions), we get the revenue-maximizing b as well as the LTC z_js, as discussed above.

While the expression for $\dfrac{dR}{\partial b}$ is long, in the sense of having many terms, it is analytically an elementary form. All the terms are merely simple arithmetic or exponential combinations of variables and known parameters. It may prove desirable, however, in view of the length of some of the derivative expressions, to try using numerical differentiation. This will be especially true later, when costs, congestion, and other terms are added on to revenue, and the enlarged expression is maximized. Use of numerical differentiation may save some tedious hours of work. However, care should be taken, as numerical derivatives can sometimes be quite inaccurate. Samples should be checked periodically against analytic evaluations.

Looking Forward

This completes the discussion of our example, as well as this basic chapter on rail line optimization. In the next chapter, we extend what has been done here to show how other terms, such as right of way land costs and congestion, might be handled by the analysis. This is a rather simple matter—since once we have expressed the dependence of these terms on the line path, we can merely add the new effects on to the revenue term and maximize the total net benefits with respect to line location parameters (and access points—in the LTC access case). Therefore, the extension of what has been done here to include even the totality of the effects mentioned in Chapter 2 is, in principle, a trivial matter as far as the optimization methodology goes. What calls for resourcefulness on the part of the planner is to model the various costs and benefits as functionals of the rail path. It is to this end that the examples of the next chapter are directed. The next chapter also deals with other issues, such as locational constraints, some of which call for modifications of the basic methodology developed here.

BIBLIOGRAPHY FOR CHAPTER 4

Akhiezer, N.I. 1962. *The Calculus of Variations*. Trans. A.H. Frink. New York: Blaisdell Publishing Co.

Arden, B., and K. Astill. 1970. *Numerical Algorithms*. Reading, Mass.: Addison-Wesley Publishing Co.

Bellman, R., and S. Dreyfus. 1962. *Applied Dynamic Programming*. Princeton, N.J.: Princeton University Press.

Boyce, D., and W.B. Allen. 1972. "Interim Report" (for the Urban Mass Transportation Administration). Offset.

Esgolc, L.E. 1962. *Calculus of Variations*. Reading, Mass.: Addison-Wesley Publishing Co.

Foster, C.D., and M.E. Beesley. 1963. "Estimating the Social Benefit of Constructing an Underground Railway in London." *Royal Statistical Society Journal*, pp. 46–93.

Gannett Fleming Corddry and Carpenter, Inc.; Bellante, Clauss, Miller and Nolan, Inc. 1974. "Summary Report on a Mass Transit Study for the Mass Transportation Development Program of the Delaware River Port Authority." UMTA (project no. IT-09-0009). Xerox.

Gelfand, I.M., and S.V. Fomin. 1963. *Calculus of Variations*. Trans. Richard A. Silverman. Englewood Cliffs, N.J.: Prentice-Hall.

Hadley, G. 1964. *Nonlinear and Dynamic Programming*. Reading, Mass.: Addison-Wesley Publishing Co.

Hadley, G., and M.C. Kemp. 1971. *Variational Methods in Economics*. Amsterdam: North-Holland Publishing Co.

Intrilligator, M.D. 1971. *Mathematical Optimization and Economic Theory*. Englewood Cliffs, N.J.: Prentice-Hall.

Lancaster, K. 1968. *Mathematical Economics*. New York: Macmillan Co.

※ *Chapter 5*

Optimal Rail Location:
Further Analysis

INTRODUCTION

In Chapter 4, we discussed the basic methodology for locating the optimal rail line—under two access assumptions. The mathematical techniques were illustrated by dealing with the case of finding the revenue-maximizing line. As indicated at the end of Chapter 4, the methodology is fundamentally unchanged when other cost and benefit terms are added in order to formulate the full welfare expression.

In order to see this, it may be helpful to have examples of other terms, expressed so as to show their dependency on the path of the rail line, f. Accordingly, we derive, in the next two sections, models of congestion benefits and right of way land costs that show the relation between the size of each of these terms and the rail path. These models serve the purpose of illustrating for two rather different kinds of effects how the planner is to make this connection between the rail path and the size of various cost or benefit terms.

In each of the cases, one could set up a more sophisticated (and accordingly more complex) model—or a grosser, less sophisticated one. The purpose of these sections is not to derive the definitive models for these effects. Indeed, such models do not, in a practical sense, exist. Rather, these sections aim at illustrating this model-building process; the number and degree of sophistication of models actually used in any practical situation will depend on such considerations as the amount of resources available to collect and process data, how much lead time one has to complete the planning task, and so forth.

Next, we deal with a rather different set of considerations. These are geographical constraints on the path the line may take. Two varieties of constraints are considered. The first type calls for the line to take a given path over one or more links—for example, over a bridge or a segment of the right of way of a highway. The second type calls for the line not to enter certain geographic areas—for example, towns that pass ordinances against the line's intrusion, or inviolate areas such as state forests or parks, and the like.

The final section deals with a variety of important issues related to optimal path selection. Topics dealt with are rotating the coordinate axes of reference, searching over endpoints (x_e values), deciding whether to build a new line, use of existing rights of way, rail location within more than one corridor, sensitivity analysis, and unquantifiable cost-benefit terms.

MODELING CONGESTION

Here we show mathematically the linkages between the upsurge of demand for the rail line, the resulting rise in the average speed of traffic for all those still using the roads, and the savings in time and vehicle operating costs (i.e., the congestion benefits) stemming from this increased velocity. Having done it in Chapter 4, we know that it is easy to demonstrate the dependence of demand on the path of the rail line. This fills in the initial link of the chain, allowing us to express congestion benefits as a function of the parameters of the line's equation.

While some pains have been taken to reduce the volume of algebraic manipulation in the congestion model below, there is much of this that still, inevitably it seems, must remain. The concepts, however, are rather elementary, and the degree of mathematical sophistication slight. Therefore, the reader should have little trouble following the twists and turns of the model.

One could increase the accuracy and sophistication of the model (and hence its complexity and data requirements) in many ways. Some of these are pointed out in the course of developing the equations; others are held until the end of the section.

The model of this section was developed independently of similar work by others. Subsequent to its development, however, it came to light that, in the appendix to the article by Foster and Beesley (1963), a set of calculations are made for London's Victoria Line that are very similar to the equations set out here. Indeed, after perusing their work, my own thinking on a few points was clarified. A debt is accordingly acknowledged. A major difference between their work and the model of this section, however, is that they deal with a rail line to be built over a known, fixed path, while our work proceeds on the basis that location is not known. Accordingly, their work consists of doing arithmetic computations for the proposed Victoria Line, while ours consists of deriving an equation to be maximized over a choice of rail paths.

The starting point for the congestion model is to predict how many auto and bus users will stop making trips by these modes, switching over to the line instead. By ascertaining how many people will make the switch, it is then possible, using vehicle occupancy factors and other parameters, to estimate how many vehicles and ultimately how many vehicle miles will be removed from the roadways of the rail line corridor. This enables us to calculate the rise in average speed and, hence, the total time and vehicle operating cost savings (i.e., congestion benefits). But lest we get ahead of our story, let us first look at the problem of predicting the decrease in the number of auto and bus users. One must bear in mind, as always, that we are dealing with an as yet unbuilt line.

Decline in the Number of Auto and Bus Users

One way to predict this decline is to transfer from a similar situation two equations, one for auto use and the other for bus use. These would be estimated as usual from the actual experience of another city or from another part of the same metropolitan area under study. Or they might be estimated from survey data. In any case, the costs by all modes would appear as explanatory variables.

However, we pursue an alternative course here, which is to use the already estimated rail demand function and to make an estimate (most likely from survey data) of the fraction of users who are replacing auto and bus trips to work with trips on the line. Assuming demand for the line to be of the c logit form, we have demand in the jth tract given by:

$$q_j = [cq_j^*]/[1+\exp(-O_j+kL_j)] \qquad (5.1)$$

Total ridership is

$$\sum_{j=1}^{N} q_j = \sum_{j=1}^{N} [cq_j^*]/[1+\exp(-O_j+kL_j)]$$

Taking as estimable parameters:

s_1 = share of total line users who were auto users
s_2 = share of total line users who were bus users

then the total number of auto and bus users who become line users is:

$$a'_1 = s_1 \sum_{j=1}^{N} [cq_j^*]/[1+\exp{(-O_j+kL_j)}]$$

= number of auto users taken off the road by the line;   (5.2)

$$a'_2 = s_2 \sum_{j=1}^{N} [cq_j^*]/[1+\exp(-O_j+kL_j)]$$

= number of bus users taken off the road by the line.   (5.3)

It is a simplification, in terms of the number of demand functions we must keep track of and write down, to use s_1 and s_2 times total line demand, rather than using a separate demand equation for auto and bus use. Therefore, we have chosen to illustrate the methodology of this section in that way. There is little difference in the basic analytics; under either procedure, a'_1 and a'_2 depend on L_j (line costs), which depends on the parameters of the line's geographic equation.

As a simple extension, we might have the fraction of auto and bus users vary with the census tract. In this case, we need a whole set of s_{1j} and s_{2j} shares, one for each $j=1, \ldots, N$. The most likely source of data is, as before, a survey.

In this section, we will look at the decrease in congestion due to the decline in car and bus use. In the analysis, we take as negligible, and hence ignore, any decongestion resulting from decreased use of motorcycles or bicycles (these people switching over to rail use). We also ignore any decongestion benefits accruing to motorcyclists and bicyclists from a general speedup in traffic, again on the grounds that it is negligible.

Four Vehicle Classes and Their Vehicle Occupancy Ratios

Following basically the classification scheme employed in the calculations of Foster and Beesley (1963), we divide all road vehicles into autos, buses, commercial vehicles (trucks, etc.), and public service vehicles (police, ambulance, etc.). The average number of people per vehicle is the occupancy ratio. We define the following ratios, one for each vehicle class (note that here, as well as below, "cv" is used for "commercial vehicle" and "psv" for "public service vehicle").

a''_1 = auto occupancy factor for vehicles in use on an average day (people per car)

a''_2 = bus occupancy factor for vehicles in use on an average day (people per bus)

a''_3 = cv occupancy factor for vehicles in use on an average day (people per cv)

$a_4'' =$ psv occupancy factor for vehicles in use on an average day (people per psv)

Frequently in this section, we shall use the subscripts 1,2,3, and 4 to differentiate a parameter according to the auto, bus, cv, and psv vehicle classes, respectively. Also, as an aid to following the algebraic manipulations, the units of measurement of newly defined parameters follow the definitions and are generally enclosed in parentheses, as above. The phrase, "on an average day," used frequently below, means that while occupancy ratios might vary over the year, what we want is the over time mean for a single day. If we limit our calculations, as we do here, to work trips, then this average should preponderantly reflect the occupancy factors during the work days. Weekend days could figure into this average, but they should be given much less than 2/7 weight because of the comparatively small number of people who work then.

The occupancy factors needed relate only to vehicles in use on an average day in the line corridor. The term "line corridor," as used in this section, should be taken as meaning the area that benefits from a decline in road congestion after the line goes into operation. In short, it is the area of interest for studying decongestion. Its geographical extent consists more or less of the residential collection shed and downtown distribution area of the line—that is, all places to which people would have driven had they not taken the line.

The regional traffic planning commission would be the body most likely to have or to be responsible for ascertaining the values of a_1'', a_2'', a_3'', and a_4''.

The Decline in the Number of Vehicle Trips
Made on the Roads

It is now an easy step to estimate the number of car and bus trips that no longer will be made on the roads of the line corridor. Recall that a_1' and a_2' represent the number of former auto and bus users now making work trips on the line. Define:

$a_1 =$ average daily number of car trips no longer being made on the roads of the line corridor (units = number of car trips per day)

$a_2 =$ average daily number of bus trips no longer being made on the roads of the line corridor (units = number of bus trips per day)

"Daily" indicates all days of the year, not just work days.

Now, if the average bus occupancy factor is 25, and 2,500 people decide day after day not to take the bus to or from work, then it seems reasonable to conclude that about $2 \times 2500/25 = 2 \times 100 = 200$ bus trips are going to be stopped each working day. Similarly, if the auto occupancy factor is 1.2, and 12,000 former auto drivers stop making work trips by car, then we may conclude that the roads will be relieved of about $2 \times 10,000 = 20,000$ auto trips on each working day.

If we assume the annual proportion of working days to be, say, 250/365 = 50/73, then, using the above examples, the average daily number of bus and of auto trips that the roads are relieved of are (100) [(2)(50/73)] and (10,000) [(2)(50/73)], respectively. Define:

c_f = conversion factor from the number of vehicles removed from the streets to the average daily number of trips eliminated from the line corridor

In the above example, c_f equals 2(50/73). We can now write the following equations for a_1 and a_2:

$$a_1 = (c_f) \, a_1'/a_1'' \tag{5.4}$$

$$a_2 = (c_f) \, a_2'/a_2'' \tag{5.5}$$

Were we explicitly considering nonwork trips as well as work trips, we would have predictions (through, perhaps, an abstract mode equation) of the number of nonwork auto and bus person trips to be eliminated when the line would start operations. It would then be necessary only to convert these person trips into the average daily number of vehicle trips eliminated by the line (by first using vehicle occupancy factors and then averaging over all days). The resultant number of such trips would then be added to a_1 and a_2 above.

Average Length of Trip—For Vehicles Eliminated from the Road

Now that we have an estimate of the average daily number of car and bus trips eliminated through the operation of the line, we can easily determine the number of car and bus vehicle miles that are eliminated. For this we need the following definitions:

ℓ' = mean length of the eliminated journeys (in miles)
ad = mean length of access distance to the line by all line users who are former auto or bus users (in miles)

Taking the difference between ℓ' and ad gives us the net roadway distance saved every time a worker gains access to and uses the line instead of using a bus or car. Let this net distance be called ℓ, so that:

$$\ell = \ell' - ad \tag{5.6}$$

Now the calculation of vehicle miles eliminated is straightforward. With a_1 commuter car trips and a_2 commuter bus trips eliminated on an average day, we see that $a_1\ell'$ and $a_2\ell'$ car and bus miles, respectively, are eliminated. However, an access trip to the line must now be made. It seems reasonable to reduce by $(a_1)(ad)$ and $(a_2)(ad)$ the number of eliminated car and bus miles, respectively. This implicitly assumes that people who formerly drove to work, for example, with 1.2 persons per car and on 50/73rds days of the year, will also do this in reaching the line stations. Similarly, former bus users, say with twenty-five persons per bus and trips on 50/73rds of the days, are assumed to reach the line by bus, with the same occupancy and frequency data pertaining. (If these implicit assumptions are not met, it is easy enough to alter the model as desired.) In sum, then, total auto vehicle miles are reduced by $a_1\ell$ miles on an average day, and bus vehicle miles are similarly reduced by $a_2\ell$ miles, where ℓ is defined in (5.6).

There are two ways to approach the measurement of ℓ' and ad. The simplest, used here, is merely to make an estimate of ℓ' based on survey data or to make an educated guess of who will ride the line (and how long their current trip is). The access distance measure, ad, could be taken from experience with other rail lines. This approach takes ℓ' and ad (hence ℓ) as known parameters.

A more complicated, but perhaps more exact, procedure involves modeling ℓ' and ad as dependent on the path of the line. The path of the line determines how many users in each tract will use the rail facility. Accordingly, ℓ' is affected according to the mix of users close to or far from the CBD, and ad is affected according to the mix of users located close to or far from the line. To model this dependence for ℓ', one need only compute an ℓ' measure for each tract; call them ℓ_j. These give the over the road distance from the tract's centroid to the CBD—with some allowance for long-run users, whose preline commuting pattern is different. We then take a weighted sum of the ℓ'_j with weights $= (s_1+s_2)q_j =$ the number of line users in each tract who are former bus or car users. The basic dependence on the rail path comes, of course, because the q_j vary with the equation of the line.

The dependence of ad on the rail path is even more obvious. The access distance from the jth tract to the rail line $y=f(x)$, when access is at the point $(z_j, f(z_j))$, for example, is merely $\sqrt{(x_j-z_j)^2 + (y_j-f(z_j))^2}$. This is a familiar expression, illustrative of the Ritz method case. Again, we multiply these access distances by the weights $(s_1+s_2)q_j$, which also depend on the path $y=f(x)$. These complications won't be incorporated formally here; however, they seem worthy of the reader's attention.

Car Equivalence

We have now progressed to the stage of being able to represent analytically the total auto and bus vehicle miles that are eliminated from the road network through the operation of the line. These are $a_1\ell$ and $a_2\ell$ miles, respectively. (The dependence of these upon the path of the line can be shown by successively substituting equations (5.2) through (5.6) into $a_1\ell$ and $a_2\ell$.)

Now we must combine the effects of the reduced number of car and bus vehicle miles, in order to show the total effect on the average speed of the vehicles still using the line corridor. This is a simple matter. Sharp (1967) points out the results of testing by Road Research Laboratories (in England), which show that, for purposes of speed-flow calculations (such as ours), one bus can be taken as the equivalent of three cars. This figure is also used in the work of Foster and Beesley (1963). However, as the relative size and maneuverability of cars versus buses may differ in England versus any other country, some caution is indicated in using this British result elsewhere.

A similar note of caution must be sounded with respect to employing Foster and Beesley's figures of 1.65 and 3.0 as the car equivalence for commercial and public service vehicles (respectively). In the computations below, these British results are used without alteration; however, traffic engineers in the country and region of interest should be consulted in any actual application.

Let the number of car equivalent vehicle miles eliminated on an average day by the operation of the line be denoted AB. AB is measured in units of car equivalent vehicle miles per day and is given by the following equation:

$$AB = (a_1 + 3a_2)\ell \qquad (5.7)$$

Inventory of Vehicles in Use—Number of Vehicles Operating in the Line Corridor on an Average Day—Without the Line

The next series of steps calls for finding the total number of car equivalent vehicle miles driven by all vehicles on an average day in the line corridor. Then we can relate this to AB, the reduction by the line of such car equivalent vehicle miles, and see the effect on average speed.

The first step is to obtain for each vehicle class the number of vehicles operating in the line corridor on an average day prior to the construction of the line. These data are garnered from traffic counts. Our inventory produces:

T'_1 such cars
T'_2 such buses
T'_3 such commercial vehicles
T'_4 such public service vehicles

Next, our traffic survey must produce either the mean length of journey or, more directly, the total vehicle miles driven—in the corridor—for each of the four vehicle classes. In Foster and Beesley (1963), the survey produced the former.

**Mean Length of Journey in the Line
Corridor (on an Average Day) for Each
Vehicle Type—Without the Line**
Define the following, for $i = 1,2,3,4$:

ϕ_i = daily mean length of journey for vehicles of the ith class in use in the line corridor—without the line (miles per day)

From these average journey lengths and from the vehicle inventory, we can quickly derive by multiplication the total number of car equivalent vehicle miles driven in the line corridor on an average day—without the line.

**Total Number of Car Equivalent Vehicle
Miles Driven in the Line Corridor (on an
Average Day)—Without the Line**
For $i=1,2,3,4$, let:

T_i = total number of car equivalent vehicle miles driven on an average day in the line corridor by the ith vehicle class—without the line (in car equivalent miles)

Then it is immediately obvious that the following equations hold:

$$T_1 = (T'_1)(\phi_1) \tag{5.8}$$

$$T_2 = 3(T'_2)(\phi_2) \tag{5.9}$$

$$T_3 = 1.65(T'_3)(\phi_3) \tag{5.10}$$

$$T_4 = 3(T'_4)(\phi_4) \tag{5.11}$$

Letting T represent the total number of such car equivalent vehicle miles across the four vehicle classes, we obviously have:

$$T = T_1 + T_2 + T_3 + T_4 \tag{5.12}$$

Note that AB/T represents the share of these total car equivalent vehicle miles that are eliminated under operation of the line. This ratio is important for deriving the increase in the speed of the traffic that remains once the line is operating. We turn to the speed question next.

Average Speed Change in the Line Corridor

Let us suppose that without the line, s represents the average speed (in miles per hour) of all vehicles in the area of interest as measured by a traffic study. Now we know that there is a $100(AB/T)$ percent decline in car equivalent vehicle miles driven on an average day. Suppose that for every 1 percent drop in such car equivalent vehicle miles in the area on interest, there is an e_1 percent rise in speed—from the level s. That is, let e_1 represent an elasticity between car equivalent vehicle miles driven on an average day in the area of interest and speed (for speeds in the neighborhood of s).

In any good planning effort, providing such an elasticity measure should be the responsibility of the regional highway or traffic department. One way to obtain e_1 is to study a sample of road links representative of those in the line corridor. One would note the effect of speed when the total number of vehicles on the roads drops. This would yield a series of elasticities; taking the relevant weighted average (perhaps weighting according to mean flow), produces e_1.

Let s' be the average speed of all vehicles in the area of interest once the line is introduced. Then it is clear that

$$s' = s[e_1(AB/T) + 1] \tag{5.13}$$

where s' is measured in miles per hour.

Time Savings and the Value of Time Saved

Now we can easily derive the aggregate yearly time saved, and the value of this time savings, for all those operating motor vehicles in the area of interest. The time savings for a journey of mean length by one vehicle on an average day is $(\varnothing_i/s - \varnothing_i/s')$ hours. And in each ith class vehicle there are a_i'' persons (the vehicle occupancy factor). One might conclude that the number of person hours saved for people in the ith vehicle class is therefore $(\varnothing_i/s - \varnothing_i/s')\,[(T_i')(a_i'')]$, the term in brackets representing the number of people each saving $(\varnothing_i/s - \varnothing_i/s')$ hours. While this holds for $i=3$, 4, it is only an approximation for buses and cars $(i=1,2)$.

To see this, recall that a'_1 of the auto users and a'_2 of the bus users become line commuters, with a road journey length on an average day of $(c_f)(ad)$ miles (not $\emptyset_1$ or $\emptyset_2$ miles, respectively). We conclude that while total time savings is

$$(\emptyset_i/s - \emptyset_i/s') [(T'_i) (a''_i)] \tag{5.14}$$

hours on an average day for $i=3$, 4, it is

$$(\emptyset_i/s - \emptyset_i/s')[(T'_i)(a''_i) - a'_i] + \left| \frac{(c_f)(ad)}{s} - \frac{(c_f)(ad)}{s'} \right| [a'_i] \tag{5.15}$$

hours on an average day for $i=1,2$. Of course, we need only multiply these expressions by 365 (or perhaps 366) in order to get the hours saved per year.

To convert hours saved into dollar values, we need value of time (VOT) measures. Let VOT_i be the value of time (in dollars per person hour) for users of ith class vehicles. For car and bus users, a natural source for obtaining VOT measures is to use the values implicit in a modal demand function. See Chapter 3 for a discussion of how to derive VOT measures for working commuters by finding the quotient of time and money cost regression coefficients in the line demand function.

For cv and psv operators, the most natural measure of VOT is the operator's gross wage. The gross wage is taken here to mean the total cost of employing the worker—including provision of uniforms, payment of Social Security tax, and any other attendant costs borne by the employer. The legitimacy of using the gross wage measure for VOT hinges on whether the time saved from the traffic speedup can be used by the employer to either increase production or reduce costs. Other standard economic assumptions must also be made; see Harrison and Quarmby (1969) for the details.

Note that while the discussion here is in terms of the value of saving time for people, there may also be gains from saving vehicle time. Such gains are especially likely to accrue to firms using a large number of vehicles—such as the bus company, a large trucking firm, and so forth. With traffic generally moving faster, these firms may not need as many vehicles to provide any given level of service. This source of gain, while basically dependent on the number of vehicle hours saved (for which we have convenient expressions above) will not be pursued in the mathematics here.

With the (VOT_i) measures, we can now express the money value of the time savings component of congestion benefits. Let I_i be the total yearly value of time saved due to the operation of the line, for people riding in ith class vehicles. Then it is immediately clear from the discussion above that for $i=1,2$:

$$I_i = (365)\ (\text{VOT}_i)\ [(\phi_i/s\ -\ \phi_i/s')\ ((T_i')\ (a_i'')\ -a_i')$$
$$+ ((c_f)\ (ad)/s\ -\ (c_f)\ (ad)/s')a_i']\quad (5.16)$$

and for $i=3,4$:

$$I_i = (365)\ (\text{VOT}_i)\ (\phi_i/s\ -\ \phi_i/s')\ (T_i')(a_i'')\qquad\qquad (5.17)$$

Since we have thus far only defined a_i' for $i=1,2$, we now set $a_3'=a_4'=0$ for the sake of convenience. This allows us to collapse equations (5.16) and (5.17) into a single equation, valid for all i. This single equation is simply (5.16), which now holds for $i=1,\ldots,4$!

Let I be the total savings over all vehicle classes. That is:

$$I = I_1 + I_2 + I_3 + I_4 \qquad\qquad\qquad\qquad\qquad (5.18)$$

We can now define I in terms of the parameters of the rail path and the other parameters developed in this section. To do this we substitute into equation (5.18) equations (5.16) and equations (5.2) through (5.7). That is,

$$I + \sum_{i=1}^{4} (365)(\text{VOT}_i)[(\phi_i/s\ -\ \phi_i/s')((T_i')(a_i'')\ -\ a_i')$$
$$+ \left(\frac{(c_f)(ad)}{s}\ -\ \frac{(c_f)(ad)}{s'}\right)a_i']\quad (5.19)$$

Further, substituting equations (5.4) through (5.7) into equation (5.13), we have:

$$s' = s[1+e_1c_f(a_1'/a_1''+3a_2'/a_2'')(\ell'-ad)/T]\qquad\qquad (5.20)$$

And substituting equations (5.2) and (5.3) into equation (5.20), we obtain the dependence of s' on the path of the rail line:

$$s'=s\left| 1+(e_1c_f(\ell'-ad)/T)\ (s_1/a_1'' + 3s_2/a_2'')\right.$$
$$\left.\left(\sum_{j=1}^{N} [cq_j^*]/[1+\exp(-O_j+kL_j)]\right)\right|\quad (5.21)$$

where, of course, L_j depends on the equation of the rail path. The path of the rail line not only affects I through s_i' as shown explicitly in equation (5.21), but also through the a_1' and a_2' entries in equation (5.19). Substituting equations (5.2) and (5.3) into equation (5.19) to show this latter dependence, we get:

$$I = \sum_{i=1}^{4} (365)(VOT_i) \Big| (\varnothing_i/s - \varnothing_i/s')((T_i')(a_i'') -$$

$$s_i \sum_{j=1}^{N} [cq_j^*]/[1+\exp(-O_j+kL_j)]) + ((c_f)(ad)/s - (c_f)(ad)/s')$$

$$\Big(s_i \sum_{j=1}^{N} [cq_j^*]/[1+\exp(-O_j+kL_j)]) \Big| \quad (5.22)$$

where we define $s_3=s_4=0$.

Finally, to show the full dependency of I upon the path of the line, we substitute equation (5.21) into equation (5.22). Since the substitution is straightforward but lengthy, we will not show it here. In such an expression, however, I is expressed as a function of the crucial L_j variables as well as of known parameters—these being: VOT_i, $\varnothing_i$, s, T_i', a_i'', s_i, c, q_j^*, O_j, k, c_f, ad, e_1, ℓ', T, as well as C_{0j}, C_{1j}, and C_{2j} from the total cost expression.

Note that I is differentiable in L_j so long as $s' \neq 0$, a condition that is sure to be satisfied. Therefore, we can maximize I (or $R+I$—net benefits, so far) by differentiating it with respect to the parameters of the rail line equation. These parameters can either be $\underline{P}$—if LTC access and the Ritz method are used—or $[v_b, v_1, \ldots, v_{Nb}, v_e]$—if vertical access and the Euler method are used.

If we assume LTC access and therefore a smooth rail line with equation $y=f(x,\underline{P})$, where $\underline{P}$ is the vector of equation parameters, then we have the usual expression for total rail cost (see equation (4.12)):

$$L_j = C_{0j} + C_{1j} \sqrt{(x_j-z_j)^2+(y_j-f(z_j,\underline{P}))^2} +$$

$$C_{2j} \int_0^{z_j} \sqrt{1+\Big(\frac{\partial f(x,\underline{P})}{\partial x}\Big)^2} \, dx \quad (5.23)$$

We need only to substitute this into equations (5.21) and (5.22) in order to get I as a function of known quantities (such as VOT_i, $\varnothing_i$, etc.) and the vector of unknown parameters, $\underline{P}$. We can then add this congestion benefits expression to the revenue equation of Chapter 4 and maximize total benefits $(R+I)$ with respect to $\underline{P}$. We do this by setting the total partial of $(R+I)$ equal to 0, as discussed in Chapter 4. (Note, of course, that I is differentiable and so is $(R+I)$.) These first order conditions replace equation (4.17), and they are solved simultaneously with equation (4.18), the cost minimizing conditions. This simultaneous solution yields the optimal $\underline{P}$ and the optimal set of z_js, the abscissa values of the access points. All of this follows exactly the lines of analysis set forth in Chapter 4—that is, $(R+I)$ is handled no differently than R.

If, instead of LTC access, the vertical access assumption is made and the Euler method of solution is used, then we merely use equations (5.21) and (5.22) in conjunction with equations (4.4) through (4.6). These three expressions give access plus line haul costs for type A, B, and C tracts—that is, they give L_j^A, L_j^B, and L_j^C. Merely substitute in the correct form of the total cost formula for each j and sum over all js (hence over all three types of tracts). This yields congestion benefits (I) as a function of the set of rail line vertex ordinate values $[v_b, v_1, \ldots, v_{Nb}, v_e]$. The basic analytics from here on out are the same for maximizing $(R+I)$ as for R, and the reader is referred to Chapter 4 for that discussion.

We turn to considering the savings in vehicle operating costs that comes as a result of decongestion.

Savings in Vehicle Operating Costs

These savings can be quite substantial. Foster and Beesley (1963) find that they represent about 30 percent of the very large decongestion benefits of the Victoria Line. (Time savings account for 70 percent.) As mentioned in Chapter 2, the main vehicle operating costs that are affected by speed of traffic are gas, maintenance and repairs, and tire expenditures. Since the average speeds we are likely to deal with are probably under thirty-five miles per hour (in Foster and Beesley's London study, average velocity was around ten to eleven miles per hour), the first two cost items fall with rising speed while the third item rises. On balance, the effects are usually favorable—that is, total operating costs fall.

Let CPM_i be the mean per mile cost of gas, tires, and maintenance and repairs (in dollars per mile) for vehicles in the ith class. And let us relate for each vehicle class the percentage rise in speed to the percentage fall in CPM_i by an elasticity measure, e_{2i}. That is, let $e_{2i} =$ (percentage change in CPM_i)/(percentage change in speed—from s).

While we have taken the relation between speed and cost as being a double log or constant elasticity form (at least within the observed range of variation), we needn't postulate this simple a connection. Similarly, we may opt for a more complex nexus between total car equivalent vehicle miles and speed than is provided by using the e_1 elasticity measure above. However, for purposes here of mathematical exposition, we use these relations.

Now since $(s'-s)/s$ gives the percentage change in speed for vehicles of all classes, it is immediate that $CPM_i([s'-s]/s)e_{2i}$ represents the per mile operating cost savings (in dollars per mile) for ith class vehicles.

We have only to multiply this per mile savings by the number of annual vehicle miles driven in order to get the aggregate reduction in yearly operating costs. For cars and buses ($i=1,2$), this annual vehicle mile figure is simply $365(T_i'\phi_i - \ell a_i)$. For cvs and psvs ($i=3,4$) it is $365(T_i'\phi_i)$. Recall that for $i=1,2$: $a_i = c_f a_i'/a_i''$, and that for $i=3,4$ we have defined $a_i'=0$. Defining J_i as the total annual vehicle operating costs saved by the speedup of traffic due to the presence of the line, for vehicles in the ith class, we have for all i:

$$J_i = 365\left(\frac{s'-s}{s}\right)(e_{2i})(CPM_i)(T_i'\phi_i - \ell c_f a_i'/a_i'') \tag{5.24}$$

Letting J be the corresponding total cost saving across all vehicle classes, we have:

$$J = J_1 + J_2 + J_3 + J_4 \tag{5.25}$$

Showing the dependence of J on the path of the rail line is easy. The major influence is probably through the s' term, though a_1' and a_2' also play a part. Substituting equations (5.2), (5.3), (5.6), (5.21) and (5.24) into equation (5.25), we get:

$$J = 365\sum_{i=1}^{4}(e_1 c_f(\ell'-ad)/T)(s_1/a_1'' + 3s_2/a_2'')$$

$$\left(\sum_{j=1}^{N}[cq_j^*]/[1+\exp(-O_j+kL_j)]\right)(e_{2i})(CPM_i)$$

$$\left(T_i'\phi_i - [(\ell'-ad)c_f/a_i'']s_i\sum_{j=1}^{N}[cq_j^*]/[1+\exp(-O_j+kL_j)]\right) \tag{5.26}$$

It is clear that J is differentiable with respect to L_j, and so it is differentiable with respect to the parameters of the line. As discussed above for the time savings term, I, the method for maximizing J (or $R+I+J$ = net benefits, so far) is very clear and has already been adequately discussed. Also pointed out more than once before is the fact that our analysis is a static one and has dealt only with work trips. The usual comments about the need for considering nonwork trips and for taking discounted streams of I and J over time—in which the parameters of these expressions are allowed to be temporally variant—apply here as well.

Further Extensions of the
Congestion Model

One basic idea for increasing the accuracy (and complexity) of the above decongestion-measuring model is to break the line corridor into zones (perhaps concentric circles around the CBD) of varying traffic speed and congestion. While removing vehicles from heavily congested roads may confer a substantial speed gain, removing them from roads on which the traffic is already in free flow will have little effect. (The latter may apply even at rush hours for the more ruralized regions, nearer to the fringes of the metropolitan area.)

Along the same line of thinking is the idea of separating peak from off-peak decongestion effects. While these effects won't exactly be the result of the line substituting for work versus nonwork trips (respectively), this connection may be a useful first approximation.

A third and final possibility for enlarging on the model of this section is to take account of two phenomena mentioned in Chapter 2. They are, first, that once traffic has speeded up due to the decongesting effects of the line, additional bus and auto trips will be generated (since such trips are now timewise cheaper); and, second, that some commuters who have switched over to using the line may go back to using the bus or car. Foster and Beesley (1963) ignore these effects in their calculations. However, these concerns may be dealt with by examining the relation of bus demand, car demand, and line demand to the travel time by bus and auto.

MODELING RIGHT OF WAY LAND COSTS

In modeling all effects considered so far—revenue and both congestion terms—demand has played a central role. In this section, we consider, for purposes of variety of illustration, a term in which demand plays no role, namely, right of way land costs. To link the path of the rail line to the value of a term, for effects in which demand plays a central role, we have relied upon the "trick" that demand depends upon line use cost and that line use cost can be written as depending on the line's geographical equation. This set of relations is a powerful aid to modeling, useful for showing the connection between rail path and the value of a large majority of effects mentioned in Chapter 2 (of which revenue and congestion have been illustrated above). The linking between the line's equation and the right of way land costs, through use of a double integral, will illustrate a second basic modeling "trick."

In outline, the method consists of obtaining land cost data for the corridor in which the line is to be constructed. Then one fits a regression curve to the data—giving cost as a closed form function, $C(x,y)$, of the

(x,y) coordinates. Supposing that the right of way is e feet on either side of the rail path, $y = f(x)$, we can easily express total right of way land costs as a double integral of $C(x,y)$, where the abscissa limits are $[0,x_e]$ and the ordinate limits $[f(x) - e, f(x) + e]$. Having chosen a (doubly) integrable form for $C(x,y)$, we do the indicated double integration and obtain a closed form expression in which cost depends on the parameters of the rail line.

This method for dealing with right of way land costs will be illustrated in more detail below. It may also be useful in modeling such terms as land clearing costs (which depend primarily on land features—woods, hills, homes, etc.—and hence are susceptible to being modeled in cost gradient form) and loss of owner's surplus and costs to associates (deriving a $C(x,y)$ gradient for these costs after taking a Roskill Commission style survey or after using a housing demand function to get data on losses [see Chapter 2]).

The Cost Gradient Method for Modeling Right of Way Land Costs

As mentioned above, the starting point for using the gradient method is to have a data base on the per acre (or some other areal measure) cost of land. The cost figures should be drawn, where possible, from actual market transactions and should reflect the cost to the regional transportation authority (or whomever is in charge of purchasing land for the line). Data should be drawn from any area through which the line might pass.

Using these data on location and cost as sample points, one fits an integrable regression curve, showing cost versus integrable functions of the x and y coordinates. A very simple example, which we shall use here merely for purposes of illustration, is to suppose the fitted cost function is of the form:

$$C(x,y) = b_0 - b_1 x^2 - b_2 y^2 \tag{5.27}$$

where $C(x,y)$ is the cost function, with arguments x and y. Assuming b_0, b_1, and b_2 are all positive, equation (5.27) says that land costs drop as we go out from the CBD, which is at (0,0). Further, the equal price contours of equation (5.27) are elliptical in shape if $b_1 \neq b_2$ and circular if $b_1 = b_2$.

Of course, in practice, a $C(x,y)$ function would contain many more terms in order to capture the intricacies of land price variation. While land prices generally decline as one moves from the CBD toward the rural fringe, there will be local surges in land costs around areas of particular attraction (parks, universities, etc.). For these one might add on mathematical terms that are centered around the local peak. For example, if there is a peak at (x_p, y_p), one might add terms onto the regression such as

$a_p/[1 + (x-x_p)^2]$ and $b_p/[1 + (y-y_p)^2]$. One may wish to alter the "1" in the denominator to a smaller (or larger) positive constant in order to make the local peak steeper (or less steep).

If there are many hills and troughs in the cost gradient that show some regularity, one may want to employ sine or cosine surfaces in order to better fit the undulations in the data. These surfaces would be of the general form $a \cdot \sin [h(x,y)]$ or $a \cdot \cos [h(x,y)]$, where a=constant, $h(x,y)$= some function of x and y. For example, $\sin(x^2+y^2)$ would show undulations that increase with frequency as one moves away from the CBD. $\sin(x^2+2y^2)$ shows the same thing—only with more peaks and troughs in the ordinate direction than in the abscissa.

Other amendments to equation (5.27), which will result in a better fit to the data, might be: (1) to add on higher order polynomial terms; (2) to use inverse polynomial terms—such as $1/(x+k_1)$, $1/(y+k_2)$, $1/(x+k_1)^2$, $1/(y+k_2)^2$, $1/(x+k_1)$ $(y+k_2)$, and so forth—choosing positive constants k_1 and k_2 such that all these terms are always positive (never 0) and using partial fractions to integrate any terms of the form $1/P(x)$, where $P(x)$ is a polynomial of degree greater than 2. The reader can undoubtedly think of other integrable forms that will help to follow well the peculiarities of a land cost gradient in any given situation. Since our task is not to write down all possibilities that might be useful in planning, but rather to illustrate a methodology, let us get back to the job of expressing right of way land costs as a function of the rail line equation—on the illustrative assumption that land costs follow equation (5.27).

The next step is to find total right of way land costs for any rail line—by integration. First, we must decide how wide the right of way is to be. A certain amount of space is needed on either side of the track in order to construct the line and repair it. I assume e feet on either side of the line is necessary. An alternative would be to allow e to decrease as the line approaches the CBD. This would reflect the fact that land is more expensive closer in, and so the right of way may be narrowed nearer to the central area. While the first assumption is used here, the reader will easily see from the equations below that the second can be incorporated into the methodology without much difficulty. One way is to make use of a simple width function, $w(x)$, in place of e.

Letting total right of way land costs be denoted by C_r, we have:

$$C_r = \int_{x=0}^{x_e} \int_{y=f(x)-e}^{f(x)+e} C(x,y)dydx = \int_{x=0}^{x_e} \int_{y=f(x)-e}^{f(x)+e} (b_0-b_1x^2-b_2y^2)dydx \quad (5.28)$$

where x_e = the abscissa value of the line's endpoint. Doing the first of the two indicated integrations, we have

$$C_r = \int_{x=0}^{x_e} [2eb_0 - 2eb_1 x^2 - (1/3)b_2(6e(f(x))^2 + 2e^3)]dx \qquad (5.29)$$

Now, if we are using the Ritz method, with $f(x)$ equal to a polynomial, say, then it is easy to perform the integration indicated in equation (5.29). If the Euler method is used, then $f(x)$ is a BLS path whose equation is defined on each of (N_b+2) intervals as:

$$f(x) = \left(\frac{v_b}{x_b}\right)x \qquad \text{for} \qquad 0 \leqslant x \leqslant x_b$$

$$= v_b + \frac{v_1 - v_b}{x_1 - x_b}(x - x_b) \qquad \text{for} \qquad x_b \leqslant x \leqslant x_1$$

$$= v_1 + \frac{v_2 - v_1}{x_2 - x_1}(x - x_1) \qquad \text{for} \qquad x_1 \leqslant x \leqslant x_2$$

$$\begin{matrix} \cdot & \cdot & \cdot & \cdot & \cdot \cdot \cdot & \cdots & \cdots & \cdots \cdots \\ \cdot & \cdot & \cdot & \cdot \cdot \cdot & \cdots & \cdots & \cdots & \cdots \cdots \\ \cdot & \cdot & \cdot & \cdot \cdot \cdot & \cdots & \cdots & \cdots \cdots \end{matrix}$$

$$= v_{Nb} + \frac{v_e - v_{Nb}}{x_e - x_{Nb}}(x - x_{Nb}) \qquad \text{for} \qquad x_{Nb} \leqslant x \leqslant x_e$$

To do the integration indicated in equation (5.29), we need only break up the $\int_0^{x_e} g(x)dx$ integral into the equivalent sum $\int_0^{x_b} g(x)dx + \ldots +$ $\int_{x_{Nb}}^{x_e} g(x)dx$. Then plug in the appropriate linear formula for $f(x)$ into each of the $g(x)$—integral by integral.

In general we may rewrite equation (5.29) as:

$$C_r = 2eb_0 x_e - (2/3)eb_1 x_e^3 - (2/3)e^3 b_2 x_e - 2eb_2 \int_{x=0}^{x_e} [f(x)]^2 dx \qquad (5.30)$$

Note that only the last of the four terms, involving the integral, depends on the path of the line.

For example, if we are trying to find the optimal linear rail line, $f(x) = bx$, then we find in equation (5.30) that $C_r = k' - (2/3)eb_2 x_e^3(b^2)$, where $k' = $ the first three terms on the RHS of equation (5.30). Note that $dC_r/db = -(4/3)(eb_2 x_e^3)b$ and that we get the cost-minimizing rail path between (0,0) and $x = x_e$ by setting $b = 0$. Of course, since right of way land cost (C_r) is only one term in our cost-benefit welfare function, this represents only a tendency, produced by this cost consideration, for the rail line to lie along the x axis. Other terms (revenue, congestion benefits, etc.) may pull the optimal line in other directions. And different $C(x,y)$ functions will produce different results. In any case, costs such as C_r are to be subtracted from the benefit expressions (such as R, I, J, etc.), and the net benefits maximized over all choices of line parameters.

We can now easily see that in order to get an explicit closed form (i.e., completely integrated) expression for C_r, two conditions—involving $C(x,y)$ and $f(x)$—must be met: (1) $C(x,y)$ must be integrable with respect to its y variable—in order to be able to do the first integration in equation (5.28); (2) after this integration is done and the limits of integration (which involve $f(x)$) are plugged in, then $C(x,y)$ and $f(x)$ must have been chosen so that the resulting expression is integrable in the x variable. Countless combinations of $C(x,y)$ and $f(x)$ exist that satisfy these very loose and general conditions, a couple of which are pointed out above. The reader is invited to think of other combinations. Such efforts will probably be far more productive if use is made of a good integral table!

A Final Word

This completes our discussion on modeling right of way land costs and, with it, the last of the three models of this book—showing the connection between the path of the line and the magnitude of various cost or benefit terms. While we have by no means covered all costs and benefits discussed in Chapter 2, limits of time and space forbid this from being our aim. Rather, what we have tried to impart in Chapters 4 and 5 is a set of tools and a way of thinking about or conceptualizing the optimal rail line problem so as to be able to solve it. The tools have been basically mathematical in nature. The fundamental thought process involved in all the models is to conceptualize how the size of the cost or benefit varies with the location of the line. For example, revenue depends on demand and on how far the commuter rides the line (hence the fare), congestion benefits depend on demand and on how long a vehicle trip is saved by using the line, and right of way land costs depend directly on the path of the line as well as on the costs of land and the width of the right of way. Having thus conceptualized the problem, we formalize our thoughts with a mathematical equation, showing the relation between the size of the benefit or cost term and the path of the line. This process has been repeatedly illustrated.

While endogenizing the rail line path is something new to mass transit planning, there is nothing inherently difficult about it. It does require a time input from trained professionals (economists, engineers, etc.) and some computer allocations. It may be substantially more expensive than older, cruder methods (the worst of which is the "doesn't this line look nice on the map" method—a name that involves some, but occasionally not a great amount, of facetiousness). However, it is my belief that the gains from good planning—for a facility that is as expensive as a modern rail line (construction costs alone running in the hundreds of millions and even billions of dollars) and that may last as long as fifty years, remaining in the same location as it is originally put—will easily outweigh the costs. It is my hope that the methods put forward in this book will find their way to application in the world of the rail planner.

Before concluding this book, we take up in two final sections a set of problems and considerations that may arise with some frequency in planning applications. To these we now turn.

GEOGRAPHICAL CONSTRAINTS ON THE RAIL LINE PATH

As mentioned earlier, two types of constraints are dealt with here. Type I constraints require the line to take a given path over one or more links, while type II constraints call for the line not to enter certain geographic areas (towns, state parks, etc.). We shall deal with each of these in turn, showing how to appropriately alter our optimization methodology—for both the Euler and Ritz solutions. It will be seen that to find the constrained optimum requires fairly trivial modifications of the Euler method, while the necessary changes are more substantial for the Ritz method.

Type I Constraints—The Line Must Take a Given Path over One or More Links

The path the rail line is to take may not be a matter of totally free choice. It may be constrained to run over a bridge (e.g., the Lindenwold HSL must run over the Ben Franklin Bridge in order to cross the Delaware River), to use certain tunnels through heavily populated areas, or to employ portions of the rights of way of highways or abandoned rail lines that have already been cleared of their former uses and owners.

Pictorially, the situation may be something like that shown in Figure 5–1. The double lines indicate the constrained portions of the rail path. Our job is to find the rest of the optimum rail line—between A and C and from D to somewhere on the line $x=x_e$.

With vertical access and the Euler method, this will be only trivially different from what we do in the unconstrained case. The access scheme is fixed and invariant; we need only make minor modifications on our set of grid points and on the formulas for access and line haul distance.

In the constrained case, we have a set of grid points whose abscissa values fall in the intervals (x_a,x_c) and $(x_d,x_e]$—rather than in $[x_b,x_e]$. As

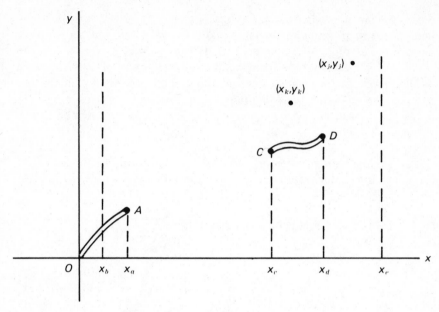

Figure 5–1. Type I Constraints.

usual, each grid point has an unknown ordinate value, $v_{(.)}$—whose value it is our object to find. The line assumes a BLS path over all unconstrained sections, as usual—and the unknown $v_{(.)}$s fully characterize and locate this BLS path. Denoting the equation of the line over the first constrained segment as $y = f_1(x)$ and over the second constrained segment as $y = f_2(x)$, we must make the natural adjustments in our access and line haul distance formulas.

For example, for tract j, located at point (x_j, y_j) in Figure 5–1, access distance is $|y_j - v_j|$, just as in Chapter 4 (assuming that we put a grid point on the vertical line $x = x_j$—as we do in Chapter 4). Line haul distance will also be the same as the summation of segment lengths expression given in Chapter 4, except with $\int_0^{x_a} \sqrt{1 + (f_1'(x))^2}\, dx$ and $\int_{x_c}^{x_d} \sqrt{1 + (f_2'(x))^2}\, dx$ replacing the corresponding sums of broken line segment lengths in the $[0, x_a]$ and $[x_c, x_d]$ intervals. Both of these integrals are known constants and present, of course, no obstacle to optimization.

As one further case of how the line haul and access distance formulas are modified under these type I constraints, take the example of a tract like tract k, located at (x_k, y_k) in the above figure—vertically above the fixed CD segment. Access distance is completely known, being $|y_k -$

$f_2(x_k)\big|$. To find the line haul distance, we use the usual sums of lengths of BLS segments between A and C plus $\int_{x_c}^{x_k} \sqrt{1+(f_2'(x))^2}\,dx$ and $\int_0^{x_a} \sqrt{1+(f_1'(x))^2}\,dx$. Again, both of these integrals are known constants.

We could continue with these cases—looking next at tracts with abscissa values between x_a and x_c, then between x_b and x_a, then less than x_b and more than x_e. But the necessary modifications should be obvious by now.

Summarizing, the procedure for finding the optimum BLS path under type I constraints, is to (1) put grid points into all the unconstrained areas; (2) consider as separate regions each of the constrained intervals, each of the alternating unconstrained intervals, and the two "half-plane" intervals where access is to the first or last station—deriving separate access and line haul distance formulas for each of these several intervals; and (3) use the access and line haul distance formulas as the basis for line cost, as shown in Chapter 4, and optimize the line path by selecting the best $v_{(\cdot)}$ vertex points.

For the BLS path and Euler method, type I constraints mean only that the number of unknown vertex points may be reduced and that the form of the distance expressions for the different tracts will show minor changes and somewhat more variety. The computer time required for solution will probably not increase; in fact, it may fall if the number of unknown $v_{(\cdot)}$s is significantly reduced. This is not true of the Ritz solution method under type I constraints—a greater number of optimization exercises must be performed, and so the need for more computer time is probably inevitable.

How do we allow for type I constraints with the Ritz method? Suppose the abscissa values of the rail line between $x=0$ and $x=x_e$ are broken into n intervals—where the $(n+1)$ interval endpoints are, in ascending order: $[x_0=0,x_1,x_2,\ldots,x_{n-1},x_n=x_e]$. In these intervals, the rail line is alternately constrained and unconstrained (or vice versa) in its path. Suppose the equation of the rail line is $y=f_i(x,\underline{P})$ in the ith interval, $[x_{i-1},x_i]$. The subscript in f_i indicates that the equation of the line may differ from interval to interval.

A few other observations are in order. $\underline{P}$ is the vector of all unknown Ritz parameters upon which the equation of the entire rail line, in all its segments, depends. (E.g., f_1 may really depend only on P_1 and P_2; f_3 may depend only on P_3, P_4, and P_5; etc.; however, we write $y=f_1(x,\underline{P})$, $y=f_3(x,\underline{P})$, etc. This is done for ease of notation.) Some f_i will be totally independent of the choice of $\underline{P}$; these are the fixed or constrained segments. Finally, since we want a continuous rail line, we require that $f_i(x_i,\underline{P}) = f_{i+1}(x_i,\underline{P})$, for all $i=1, \ldots, (n-1)$.

The most basic alterations in the Ritz methodology come in the part where we minimize access costs, rather than in the welfare maximization per se. So let us look at LTC access first.

For the jth tract, whose centroid is at (x_j, y_j), access and line haul costs to the access point $(z_j, f_1(z_j))$, located somewhere in the first interval, $[0, x_1]$, are:

$$(\text{access costs})_1 = C_{1j}\sqrt{(x_j - z_j)^2 + (y_j - f_1(z_j))^2} \tag{5.31}$$

$$(\text{line haul costs})_1 = C_{2j}\int_0^{z_j}\sqrt{1 + (f'_1(x))^2}\, dx \tag{5.32}$$

If access is to a z_j somewhere in the second interval, $[x_1, x_2]$, then:

$$(\text{access costs})_2 = C_{1j}\sqrt{(x_j - z_j)^2 + (y_j - f_2(z_j))^2} \tag{5.33}$$

$$(\text{line haul costs})_2 = C_{2j}\int_{x_1}^{z_j}\sqrt{1 + (f'_2(x))^2}\, dx +$$

$$C_{2j}\int_0^{x_1}\sqrt{1 + (f'_1(x))^2}\, dx \tag{5.34}$$

Note the differences between the formulas when z_j occurs in the first versus the second interval: (1) the access cost formula changes—in that the subscript of f_i changes—indicating a different function; (2) the line haul cost formula changes in that: (a) we now integrate from x_1 to z_j (instead of 0 to z_j), (b) we integrate to find the path length along f_2—not f_1, and (c) we add on a "constant" = the path length of f_1 in the entire first interval (we say it is "constant" because its value doesn't vary with z_j; though of course we recognize that its value may vary with $\underline{P}$). We could continue giving the access and line haul costs for each remaining interval—from 3 to n. However, the reader should have grasped the basic ideas, and we give only the costs for access to a z_j somewhere in the general ith interval:

$$(\text{access costs})_i = C_{1j}\sqrt{(x_j - z_j)^2 + (y_j - f_i(z_j))^2} \tag{5.35}$$

$$(\text{line haul costs})_i = C_{2j}\int_{x_{i-1}}^{z_j}\sqrt{1 + (f'_i(x))^2}\, dx +$$

$$C_{2j}\sum_{k=1}^{i-1}\int_{x_{k-1}}^{x_k}\sqrt{1 + (f'_k(x))^2}\, dx \tag{5.36}$$

Note that in line haul costs, for $i = 1$, we have the sum $\sum_{k=1}^{0}$, which should be interpreted to have 0 value (i.e., to be the sum of 0 terms).

To find the minimum cost z_j, for any given set of line parameters, $\underline{P}$, we must solve n simple calculus problems and check total costs at the following $(n+1)$ endpoints: $[x_b, x_1, x_2, \ldots, x_n = x_e]$—assuming only for the sake of argument that $0 < x_b < x_1$. (If $x_b \geq x_1$, then the number of intervals in which the commuter can gain access to the line is reduced—and, accordingly, so is the number of calculus solutions and endpoint checks we need to perform.) That is, we find the minimum cost z_j access value for each of the n intervals—be it an interior or an endpoint minimum, and then find the optimum LTC access value over all these candidates. We do this cost minimization for each of the n intervals, just as we did it for the single interval $[x_b, x_e]$ in Chapter 4.

Recall that the procedure set out in Chapter 4 for solving jointly for the set of LTC access points and the parameters of the line that maximize welfare (or revenue in that early exposition) runs as follows: (1) guess a value of $\underline{P}$, the parameters of the welfare-maximizing line; (2) given this $\underline{P}$, solve for the cost-minimizing set of z_j; (3) given this set of z_j, solve for a new value of $\underline{P}$—by setting the total partial derivative $dW/\partial\underline{P}$ equal to 0 and solving for $\underline{P}$. Note that $W = $ welfare $= R + I + J - C_r +$ other terms. We then iterate steps (2) and (3) until convergence. Note that this means that every time we do step (2) and we are solving a problem with type I constraints rather than no constraints at all, we must perform many extra calculus solutions and endpoint checks. This is the extra computation referred to above for the Ritz method of solution.

Step (3) is not greatly different in the unconstrained and constrained cases, though the changes should be noted. First, the revenue or, more generally, the welfare expression will depend on which of the n intervals each of the z_j lies in. This is because revenue, congestion, and many other welfare terms depend on demand, which depends on line costs; and as we have seen above, the line cost expression varies with the interval of access. Since in our iterative solution procedure we have a set of z_js before we try to solve the welfare maximizing $\underline{P}$, we can, of course, write out a single definitive (for that iteration) welfare expression. Maximizing this expression with respect to $\underline{P}$ by setting $dW/\partial\underline{P} = 0$, proceeds much as described in Chapter 4.

The only really new problem that may arise in this procedure in the case of dealing with type I constraints is when a cost-minimizing z_j value falls within the (x_b, x_e) interval at one of the endpoints of the n intervals—namely, at $x = x_1, x_2, \ldots, x_{n-2}, x_{n-1}$. At these points, the right and left hand partial derivatives of $\partial W/\partial z_j$ will, in general, differ. (To see why, note that the expressions for access and line haul cost—upon which R and other terms in W depend—have kinks at each of these points.) Recall that it is necessary to evaluate $\partial W/\partial z_j$ in order to get $dW/\partial\underline{P}$, which is needed in order to solve for P in $dW/\partial\underline{P} = 0$.

It is, in general, highly unlikely that one of a handful of kink points on a continuous rail line will turn out to be the cost-minimizing access point. Should this situation arise, however, we may employ the usual method of perturbing slightly the centroid of the offending tract, which should eliminate the problem by altering the point of access.

Type II (Nonentrance) Constraints—
The Line Cannot Enter Certain
Geographic Areas

Examples of areas that the line may not be allowed to enter are towns that pass ordinances against its intrusion, state and national parks or forests, historical sites, and other regions that are for some reason inviolate. We may also include topographic or physical features through which construction of the line may be ruled out a priori. These may include lakes, canyons, mountains, swamps, and so forth.

Having demonstrated how to deal with type I constraints, it is easy to explain how to optimize the rail path with type II constraints. This is because the method proposed here for dealing with the latter operates by reducing the problem to one with constraints of the former kind. Specifically, referring to Figure 5–2, suppose there is a nonentrance area as that marked by the cross-hatched region. And suppose that our optimal unconstrained rail line does indeed go through this forbidden territory. Then our type II constraint is a binding one, and it is suggested that the following procedure be used.

On two vertical lines (such as $x=x'$ and $x=x''$ in Figure 5–2), which bracket the cross-hatched region, mark off grid points more or less near to the nonentrance area. Connect all pairs of points that do not go through the constrained region. (These are connected by double lines in Figure 5–2.) Take each of these admissible paths in turn as a type I constrained path and solve a type I constrained optimization problem. Do this for each link around the nonentrance region. Finally, pick the type I constraint path and the rail line that gives the maximum benefit-cost surplus.

A few caveats should be noted. First, if in Figure 5–2 $x' < x_e < x''$, then we would naturally put our grid points on the vertical lines $x=x'$ and $x=x_e$ instead of on $x=x'$ and $x=x''$. Second, it will probably pay off in most cases to ignore type II constraints on the first cut at the optimization problem, allowing for them only if they prove binding. This is because of the large amount of computation that these constraints may necessitate. Third, it is quite possible that the planner will develop a "feel" for the problem and will not have to do anywhere near all possible combinations of admissible connections of grid point pairs in order to find the best one. Along these lines, it should be noted that the planner may want to try paths that bypass the nonentrance area and are not close to it (unlike *a, b,*

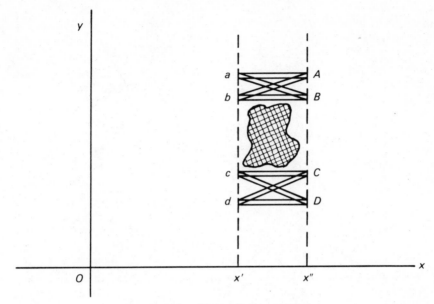

Figure 5–2.   Type II Constraints.

c, d, A, B, C, D). Also, use of constrained curvilinear sections may be desirable—in place of the linear connections of grid points shown in Figure 5–2. Finally, the reader may note the partial connection between this procedure and the basic geometry of dynamic programming.

FINAL CONSIDERATIONS

In this final section, we cover a potpourri of important issues related to optimal path selection. While it is impossible to foresee all possible issues that might come up in the use of the methodology proposed here, this section covers many that now seem important. Often the points are quite simple, though hopefully worthy of being made!

Rotating the Coordinate Axes
under LTC Access

In all cases dealt with in this book, the equation of the optimal rail line, $y = f(x)$, is a function, not a relation. This means that for any given x value there exists one and only one y value $= f(x)$. In a relation, more than one y value may be associated with a given x value. In Figure 5–3, OA is a function while OB and OC are relations.

While it is mathematically useful to limit ourselves to the class of functions when looking for the optimal rail equation, it is, nevertheless,

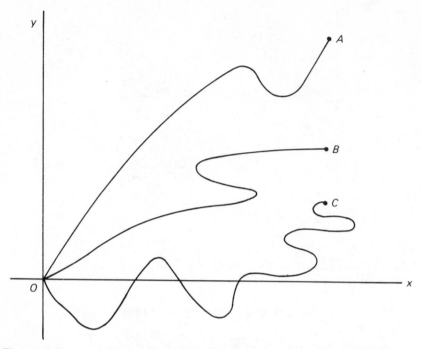

Figure 5–3.　Functions and Relations—Rotating the Coordinate Axes.

somewhat of a restriction to do so. For example, paths like *OB* will not be considered. Accordingly, one may want to rotate the *x* and *y* axes. For example, in Figure 5–3 a 90° rotation, which interchanges the *x* and *y* axes, renders *OB* a function and hence an admissible solution to the optimal rail problem. This same rotation invalidates *OA*, however, and therefore one may want to find the optimal line under more than one positioning of the coordinate axes—choosing the line that yields the greatest gain in welfare (as usual).

Of course, it is possible to dream up all kinds of snakelike curves that will not be functions under any choice of coordinate axes and, hence, will be implicitly eliminated from consideration. Path *OC* in the above figure is such an example. One should not make too much of this, however. For serving any given corridor, a relatively straight (unsinuous) radial line out from the CBD will generally be best. At least this is the implicit opinion of the mass transportation experts so far—as represented by paths that existing suburban rail lines take (for example in Philadelphia, San Francisco, New York, and Washington, D.C.). Further, too many undulations add heavily to construction costs and severely reduce the competitive edge of the line by increasing greatly the line haul time from the access point to the CBD.

Finally, it should be observed that rotation of the coordinate axes to more than one orientation is relevant only to LTC access. For vertical access, we must align the ordinate axis with the major roadways serving the line.

Searching over Endpoints

We only wish to remind the reader that while we have often considered the problem of finding the optimal rail path between the CBD at (0,0) and any point on the vertical line $x = x_e$, we must, of course, search over a grid of x_e values in order to allow a good variety of endpoint locations. One possible time-saving strategy for this is to use a fairly coarse grid of x_e values at first (say at intervals of a mile or two), and then, if one feels confident in having located the approximate vicinity of the optimal endpoint, to do a fine grid search on x_e within this vicinity.

To Build or Not to Build

We have so far discussed the optimal rail methodology in terms of selecting the best line from among alternative paths. Since we have accomplished this by maximizing a benefit-cost measure, it is apparent that we can simultaneously make the choice on whether or not to build a rail line at all, based on the computed welfare measure of the best rail line. (See Chapter 2 for a discussion of the choice of welfare criteria.)

Note, however, that even if our predictions on revenue, congestion benefits, and so forth are far off the mark (e.g., due to a bad demand forecast) we still may choose the best (or nearly the best) located rail line. This will be the case so long as our miscalculation affects all possible lines by an equal absolute amount, an equal percentage, or in some other monotonic way. While the decision on where to build the line may not be affected by such mistakes, the decision on whether to build the line can be if the errors are not offsetting, and take computed welfare across a crucial threshold.

Use of Already Owned Rights of Way and Other Government Land

Use of already owned and cleared federal, state, or local land can save a great deal of expense in terms of land purchase and community or neighborhood disruption. For example, the Lindenwold HSL was built over the right of way of an antiquated rail line. Use of highway rights of way is part of the cost-cutting strategy of the planners of the Washington, D.C., Metro.

One might try to include these cost drops in the cost gradients—as discussed above. However, it may prove inconvenient to try to model these sudden and discontinuous drops over long and narrow and perhaps winding routes. If so, one may choose to model costs without taking account of these special little rivulets of less costly land. Then, after finding the optimal line in the absence of such considerations, one would compare net benefits of this line with those of lines that use the already owned rights of way—either totally or partially.

By the way, if a line uses fixed rights of way only partially, we may want to solve an optimal rail problem with type I constraints—if the gaps between the fixed links are long enough to warrant an optimization procedure to fill them in.

Examining Several Corridors
While we have dealt so far with finding the optimal line for a single corridor, there is nothing to keep us from slicing up the metropolitan area like a pie (or in some other way) and finding the optimal rail lines within each of several corridors. Exactly what shape corridors would be useful to examine here depends on the local problems and alternatives.

Sensitivity Analysis
There may be substantial uncertainty about some of the assumptions made in the analysis (e.g., will town A exclude the line? will property taxes be used to cover the local share of the construction costs—or some other taxes?) or about the value of key parameters (e.g., discount rate, length of project life, fare parameters, congestion parameters, distributional weights, time trends on the independent variables in the demand equation, etc.). Running the optimality calculations under different options is the recommended procedure. This technique is well known, and we need not discuss it further here. It is often used in cost-benefit analyses; for example, the Roskill Commission study on the siting of the third London airport made about one hundred sensitivity analysis runs.

Unquantifiable Cost-Benefit Terms
While many of the major cost and benefit terms discussed in Chapter 2 seem quite capable of monetary quantification, some may elude such assignment of value. These effects will remain outside of the optimization methodology discussed in the preceding pages of this book. All the planner can do (perhaps with the aid of public hearings or other such fora) is to attempt to answer as best she or he can the following two questions: In which direction would inclusion of the unquantified terms pull the line? Would inclusion of the unquantified terms affect the basic desirability of building the line? These are the fundamental "where" and

"whether" problems, whose answers this book has endeavored to provide.

BIBLIOGRAPHY FOR CHAPTER 5

Foster, C.D., and M.E. Beesley. 1963. "Estimating the Social Benefit of Constructing an Underground Railway in London." *Royal Statistical Society Journal*, pp. 46–93.

Harrison, A.J., and D.A. Quarmby. 1969. "The Value of Time in Transport Planning: a Review." In *Theoretical and Practical Research on an Estimation of Time-Saving*, European Conference of Ministers of Transports, Report of the Sixth Round Table. Paris: Economic Research Center.

Quarmby, D.A. 1967. "Choice of Travel Mode for the Journey to Work: Some Findings." *Journal of Transport Economics and Policy*, pp. 273–314.

Sharp, C.H. 1967. "The Choice between Cars and Buses on Urban Roads." *Journal of Transport Economics and Policy*, pp. 104–11.

✳ Index

Wage rate
  gross, 133
  vs. VOT, 59-62
  vs. VOTF, 63-64
Walk access, in demand analysis of
  HSL, 58-59, 73, 98
Walking and waiting time costs, 9,
  98-99
Warner, S., 51, 66, 75
Washington, D.C. Metro System, 3n,
  4, 20, 27, 29, 44, 150-51
Wealth of Nations, The, 1, 60
Weisbrod, B.A., 18n, 33-34
Welfare
  function, 28, 33-34

-maximizing line, 97, 102, 123,
  146-47, 150-51
payments, reduction in, 21
Westley, G.D., 23, 43, 76n
Williams-Kloot prediction test, 70,
  85, 88-89
Williamson, H.F. and L. Moses, 59
Wilson, A.G., 43
Wise, J., C.B. Chapman and D.W.
  Pearce, 34
Work trips, in demand analysis,
  41-44, 45-48

Young, K.H. and R.E. Quandt, 43n

✳ **About the Author**

Glenn D. Westley is an economist in the project methodology division of the Inter-American Development Bank in Washington, D.C. Previously, he has acted as consultant to the Development Foundation of Turkey in Ankara, Turkey, and has worked at the U.S. Department of Housing and Urban Development. Dr. Westley has a long-standing interest in urban mass transportation problems and has spoken at the invitation of the biannual Land Economics conference on the subject of rail line location planning.